THE BIG QUESTIONS

THE BIG
QUESTIONS

JONATHAN HILL

LION

Copyright © 2007 Jonathan Hill

The author asserts the moral right
to be identified as the author of this work

A Lion Book
an imprint of
Lion Hudson plc
Mayfield House, 256 Banbury Road,
Oxford OX2 7DH, England
www.lionhudson.com
ISBN 978-0-7459-5140-9

First edition 2007
10 9 8 7 6 5 4 3 2 1 0

Acknowledgments
All scripture quotations are taken from the New Revised Standard
Version published by HarperCollins Publishers, copyright © 1989
by the Division of Christian Education of the National Council of
the Churches of Christ in the USA, and are used by permission.
All rights reserved.

The text paper used in this book has been made from wood
independently certified as having come from sustainable forests.

A catalogue record for this book is available
from the British Library

Typeset in 10/12.5 OriginalGaramond BT
Printed and bound in Great Britain
by Cox and Wyman Ltd

Contents

Introduction

Eighteen hundred years ago, the great Christian theologian Tertullian wrote:

> We do not want any searching inquiry after we possess Christ Jesus, no investigation after enjoying the gospel! With our faith, we do not want any more belief. For this is our primary faith – that there is nothing else that we should believe.[1]

Ever since Tertullian wrote these words – adding that he looked forward to watching pagan philosophers burn on judgment day – many Christians have shared his view. If you have faith in Christ, what more do you need? But many others have disagreed. They may have shared Tertullian's belief that faith in Christ is all you need for salvation, but they have rejected his conclusion that this means there is no point to asking questions about anything else. Over a thousand years after Tertullian, the Dominican theologian Thomas Aquinas commented:

> Of all human activities, the pursuit of wisdom is the most perfect, the most sublime, the most useful, and the most pleasant. It is the most perfect, because to the extent that someone gives himself up to the pursuit of wisdom, to that extent he already enjoys some portion of true happiness. 'Happy is the person who meditates on wisdom' (Ecclesiasticus 14:20). It is the most sublime, because in this way people come closest to the likeness of God, who 'has made all things in wisdom' (Psalm 104:24). It is the most useful, because by this same wisdom we arrive at the realm of immortality. 'The desire for wisdom leads to a kingdom' (Wisdom 6:20). It is the most agreeable, because 'companionship with her has no bitterness, and life with her has no pain, but gladness and joy' (Wisdom 8:16).[2]

Throughout the history of the church, Christians who have taken Aquinas' side over Tertullian's have asked – and tried to answer –

questions thrown up by their faith. Some of the questions they have addressed have been unique to Christianity, such as the question of how Christ could be both fully human and fully divine, or how God can be three persons at once. Other questions have been more universal in scope, such as why there is suffering, what hope there is for life after death, and how to live a good life. These more universal questions, and the answers to them that Christians have suggested, are the subject of this book.

Each chapter asks one of the 'big questions' and surveys some of the Christian responses to it. Some are explicitly religious, and so we shall be dipping into the philosophy of religion, the attempt to apply philosophical techniques to religious subjects; others are less so. In such a short space it is impossible even to attempt a thorough examination of either the problems thrown up by the questions or the full range of possible answers; the Christian tradition alone is far too vast for that. But I have tried to give an idea of how issues that might seem quite distinct often lead into each other: how the answer to one problem might well affect the answer to another, perhaps in ways we would not like. Sometimes I have mentioned views put forward by writers from traditions other than the Christian one, when they shed light on the problem or help to put Christian thinkers into context.

There are no easy answers to these problems. Each chapter not only describes some of the responses that have been given, but also provides some commentary – none of it definitive. Each of the figures we meet in this book developed their own views by thinking on those of the people who went before, as well as by adding their own unique contributions. The aim is to give the reader some of the tools and materials needed to do the same thing.

Perhaps the main impression one gets from even a short survey like this is just how diverse the Christian tradition is, even on subjects where we might expect Christians to agree with each other. Often, throughout history and today, churches and other Christian groups have attempted to develop or impose a 'party line' on all kinds of subjects, but in the long run, none has ever fully succeeded. In fact, there does not seem to be anything like 'the' Christian view on anything at all, even fairly fundamental things such as the nature of God. Each individual has had to develop his or her own view on these matters. That is a process that is unlikely to end any time soon.

Chapter 1

Who is God Anyway?

According to the book of Exodus, God appeared to Moses in a burning bush and told him that he was going to lead the Israelites out of slavery in Egypt. Moses, perhaps not unnaturally, expressed some reservations about this startling news. In particular, he wanted to know who was speaking to him in this unusual way:

> But Moses said to God, 'If I come to the Israelites and say to them, "The God of your ancestors has sent me to you," and they ask me, "What is his name?" what shall I say to them?' God said to Moses, 'I am who I am.' He said further, 'Thus you shall say to the Israelites, "I Am has sent me to you."'
> **Exodus 3:13–14**

That may not seem a very helpful answer; little wonder that, according to Exodus, Moses continued to hesitate for some time. But it's a question that Christians and others have asked repeatedly throughout history, and they have not always agreed on the answer. Who is God? *What* is God? What do we even mean when we use the word 'God'?

The Jewish Heritage

Christianity inherited its faith in God from Judaism. It seems likely that, originally, the Jews thought of God (or Yahweh) as 'their' god, the god of their tribe, as opposed to all the other gods that were allied to other tribes or nations. Later, they came to think of Yahweh as more powerful than all of the others. And eventually, they thought of Yahweh as the *only* god. Other 'gods' either didn't exist or were simply servants of Yahweh. This well-developed monotheism is hinted at in the passage from Exodus quoted above: when God calls himself 'I am who I am', he means, in part, that he is the ultimate reality. There is only one God, and he is greater than all other things.

In addition to this, Judaism bequeathed to Christianity several other beliefs about God. According to the book of Genesis, God created the universe, including human beings. And despite his exalted position, God was quite interested in human beings, especially those descended from Abraham. The Old Testament portrays God as constantly involved in the history of the Jews, an involvement that began when, according to Genesis 17, he made a covenant with Abraham and his descendants. God promised to make Abraham's descendants a great people and to give them the land of Canaan; in return, Abraham and his descendants were to be circumcised. God renewed and expanded the covenant with Abraham's son Isaac, and with *his* son Jacob. This identification between God and his people is expressed in the passage that follows the one from Exodus quoted above:

> God also said to Moses, 'Thus you shall say to the Israelites, "The Lord, the God of your ancestors, the God of Abraham, the God of Isaac, and the God of Jacob, has sent me to you": This is my name for ever, and this my title for all generations.'
> **Exodus 3:15**

For most Jews at the time when Christianity was first developing, that relationship between God and Israel was focused on two things. The first was the exodus, the major event described in the book of that name. As the story went, after (reluctantly) accepting the commission that God gave him in the burning bush, Moses went on to confront Pharaoh, who had enslaved the Israelites in Egypt. He eventually succeeded in securing their release, and so the Israelites fled Egypt – pursued by the minions of Pharaoh, who had changed his mind about giving up his free labour supply. But God led the Israelites in a pillar of fire and cloud, and miraculously gave them passage through the Red Sea before drowning their pursuers.

This was the great event that Jews still remember at Passover, the time when God led their ancestors out of slavery, and it reflects the Jewish faith in Yahweh as a *saving* God.

The second major element in God's relationship to Israel was the Law, which Jews believed God had delivered personally to Moses after the exodus. This, recorded in the first five books of the Old Testament, was a substantial body of legal material which the Israelites were required to observe. It's important to recognize that Jews in the early centuries of Christianity – just like modern Jews – didn't think that God's favour or grace depended upon keeping the Law. The idea wasn't that you kept the Law and then God rewarded you for it. Rather, God poured his grace upon Israel anyway, and, for Jews, keeping the Law was a grateful response to this. After all, God brought the Israelites out of Egypt first and only *then* gave Moses the Law.

Christianity inherited not only the monotheism of Judaism but also both of these concerns. For Christians, the idea of God as a saving God came to revolve around the idea that he saved his people through Christ, rather than through the exodus, although the exodus was reinterpreted as a sort of foreshadowing of Christian salvation. The passage of the Israelites through the Red Sea, for example, was understood as a prefiguring of baptism, the ceremonial washing with water by which people were initiated into the Christian religion. As for the Law, Christians at an early stage rejected the notion that it was still binding on Christians, although this shift in belief was certainly not easy: just read Paul's agonized passages on the subject, such as Romans 9–11. But Christians did retain an emphasis on morality and on leading a good life as a response to God's goodness, and even an idea that morality itself derived from God in some way. We shall look in more detail at those claims in chapters 9 and 10.

The Greek Heritage and the Spiritual God

The early Christians' view of God was also greatly influenced by other schools of thought in the ancient world, which had been arguing about God (and many other things) with each other since long before the Christians had turned up. One was Platonism, the school of thought inspired by the writings of Plato, the great Greek philosopher of the fourth century BC. Plato had occasionally talked about 'God' (or 'the divine'), and in the early centuries of Christianity Platonists generally agreed that there was a God who was ultimately responsible for the existence and nature of the world. One of the most important themes of Plato's writings was the distinction between the physical world, which we see around us, and the intellectual world, which we cannot see but which is just as real. In fact, it is *more* real than the physical world, because physical things derive their being from intellectual ones. For the Platonists, God was part of the intellectual world, and therefore completely non-physical; he could be found – if at all – only by the mind. Another philosophical group known as the Stoics, meanwhile, offered an alternative view. They were materialists, meaning that they did not believe that anything existed that was not physical and material. But they did believe in God – they just thought that he, too, was physical, although made of a very thin and tenuous sort of matter, like fire. Finally, some philosophers didn't believe in God at all. The Epicureans, for example, were materialists like the Stoics, but they didn't believe in any divine entities. But they were a relatively small minority and had to endure considerable criticism and even ridicule from the more pious groups.

The views of the philosophers had already influenced some strands of Judaism before the Christians came on the scene. For example, the Jewish book of Wisdom (which most Christians place in the Apocrypha) shows the influence of Greek philosophy in its depiction of God's wisdom as a quasi-independent agent of God, just as many Platonists and Stoics alike believed that God's reason (his *Logos*, in Greek) could act on his behalf in the world without God having to get his hands dirty, as it were. Philo of Alexandria, a Jewish philosopher living at around the same time as Jesus, pioneered the use of philosophical ideas and language to express the Jewish faith, and his writings were of great interest to the Christian philosophers who came later (although the pagan Platonists and others seem not to have paid him any attention).

Thus the early church saw lots of different ideas jostling for space. For example, some Christians seem to have agreed with the

Stoics that God was physical. Tertullian, who came from Carthage in the late second century and was the first great Christian thinker to write in Latin, seems to have been among them. Tertullian was deeply influenced by Stoicism, a philosophy that was especially popular in the western, Latin-speaking half of the Roman empire. It seems that the practically minded Romans liked this materialistic philosophy with its emphasis on ethics, for the Stoics had an elaborate and very rigorous system of morality. In fact, they thought that human happiness consisted solely in being virtuous. Tertullian was also a very strict moralist – so strict, indeed, that later generations of Christians have found him rather hard to stomach.

But if Tertullian was a materialist, most Christian thinkers in the early centuries were more influenced by Platonism. They thought that Plato's distinction between the lower, physical world and the higher, intellectual one fitted well with Christianity, and so most of the important Christian theologians until the Middle Ages (and even many after that) were Platonists of one degree or another. In fact, in late antiquity many people believed that the great sages of the past, although coming from different traditions, had been in basic agreement. For example, some philosophers and scholars – although not Jewish or Christian themselves – were interested in the Jewish scriptures, which they thought might contain philosophical wisdom to supplement that of Plato and others. Moses, who was believed to have written the first five books of the Old Testament, was held up as a precursor to Plato. One philosopher, Numenius, who lived in Syria in the second century, called Plato 'Moses speaking Greek' – all the more remarkable since Numenius was neither Jewish nor Christian, but a Pythagorean who venerated Plato. The upshot of all this was that, although most Christian theologians regarded Moses as a greater authority than Plato (they sometimes liked to point out that Plato lived later than Moses and probably stole most of his ideas from the earlier writer), they interpreted the Bible in a Platonist way. We shall see later how certain Platonic doctrines became incorporated into Christianity, such as the immortality of the soul and the non-physicality of God.

Materialists like Tertullian were thus in a minority among the largely Platonist Christians. Origen, who lived a few years later than

Tertullian, emphasized this point repeatedly in his works. The fact that he and others felt the need to do so suggests that many Christians thought differently – something that many may find surprising today, when most people are used to thinking of God as non-physical. But the Stoics had argued that only a physical thing can affect another physical thing. For example, if you want a ball to move, you have to push it with some physical thing (such as your hand). If God were non-physical, then he wouldn't be able to do anything, and he might as well not exist. Moreover, less philosophically aware Christians had reasons of their own for thinking God physical. The Bible never says that God is *not* physical. John 4:24 states that 'God is spirit', but what does that mean? To a materialist like Tertullian, 'spirit' just means a sort of thin matter, like fire, and is not opposed to 'body' at all. And indeed, the Greek word for 'spirit' is the same as that for 'breath', which is obviously physical. Other passages such as Colossians 1:15 or 1 Timothy 1:17 call God 'invisible', but that is compatible with being material (air is both invisible and material). The same is true of lacking flesh and bones, which according to Luke 24:39 is characteristic of spirits.

In fact, many Christians in antiquity believed not only that God was material and physical, but that he had something like a human body. The Bible, especially the Old Testament, often talks as if he does. According to Isaiah 59:1–2, God has hands, ears and a face. In Exodus 33, Moses asks to see God's glory, but is told that no one can see God's face and live; God therefore puts his hand over Moses' face while he passes, but takes it away so that Moses can see the divine back. And in Genesis 3:8, God goes walking in a garden. Many philosophically inclined Christians (such as Origen) argued that passages such as these should not be taken literally, but were simply a poetic way of talking about the spiritual, non-physical God. But many others were not so sure. To them, these passages simply confirmed Genesis 1:26, according to which God made human beings in his own image and likeness. They saw no reason not to suppose that this meant a physical image and likeness.

The two views clashed in Egypt at the end of the fourth century, in what became known as the First Origenist Controversy. The problem began with the monks who had been living in the Egyptian deserts for about a century. Many of the monks were well-educated Christians from elsewhere in the Roman empire who had come to Egypt to escape the bustle of city life and its distractions. One of the most famous was Evagrius Ponticus, who had been educated at Constantinople but ended up at Nitria. He wrote a number of books about the monastic life, which were full of the influence of Origen. But many other monks were simpler men who had grown up in the Egyptian countryside and were not familiar with sophisticated theology. They were used to taking the Bible literally, including the parts about God's body. Some had been brought up as pagans and only converted to Christianity later in life; these were used to seeing pagan idols in pagan temples, and to thinking about the divine in a correspondingly physical fashion.

The controversy blew up when Theophilus, patriarch of Alexandria (and, if the sources are to be believed, a thoroughly cynical and unscrupulous politician) tried to clamp down on Origenism, in particular the notion that God did not have a body. We are told that he was originally an Origenist himself and believed God to be incorporeal, but nevertheless decided to attack the Origenists. In AD 399 he sent a letter to all the churches and monasteries in Egypt arguing *for* Origenism, but in AD 401 he sent another one in which he changed his mind, writing that 'according to the sacred Scripture God has eyes, ears, hands, and feet, as men have; but the partisans of Dioscorus [one of the leading intellectual monks], being followers of Origen, introduce the blasphemous dogma that God has neither eyes, ears, feet, nor hands'. The controversy that followed turned quite violent, with monks loyal to Theophilus rampaging through Nitria and other strongholds of Origenism, but it only lasted for a few years because Theophilus soon turned his attention (and his ambitions) elsewhere.

It is important to understand that this controversy, like most within the church, was not just about an abstract theological point that made no difference to most people. Those involved, on both sides, felt that the very heart of their faith was at stake. The fifth-century monastic writer John Cassian described the plight of one monk, an elderly and much-respected abbot named Serapion (his name, like that of Origen himself, is both Egyptian and pagan in origin). He believed that God had a physical body like that of human beings. But a theologian from Cappadocia visited one day, and convinced him that most Christians believed otherwise. The other Origenists were delighted to see the respected Serapion abandon what they called his 'anthropomorphic' heresy, but Cassian writes:

> When we got up to give thanks, and were all offering up our prayers to the Lord, the old man was so bewildered in his mind during his prayer because he felt that the anthropomorphic image of the Godhead which he used to think of when praying was banished from his heart, that he suddenly burst into a flood of bitter tears and sobs, and threw himself to the ground and groaned loudly: 'Alas! wretched man that I am! they have taken my God away from me, and now I have none to lay hold of; and I do not know who to worship and address.'[1]

Ultimately, the 'spiritual' interpretation of the 'anthropomorphic' passages won out, and the faith of people like Serapion in a human-shaped God faded away. The issue remains alive in some quarters today, though, since The Church of Jesus Christ of Latter-day Saints (also known as the Mormons) has revived the doctrine. Joseph Smith, the founder of the Mormons, wrote in 1843:

> The Father has a body of flesh and bones as tangible as man's; the Son also; but the Holy Ghost has not a body of flesh and bones, but is a personage of Spirit. Were it not so, the Holy Ghost could not dwell in us.[2]

For Mormons, people like Serapion and other 'anthropomorphites' reflected the original beliefs of Christians, and Origen and other 'spiritualizers' were corrupting the faith with their love of Greek philosophy. And even apart from that, the old controversy is still important today for Christians simply because of the questions it raises. Grant, for the sake of argument, that the 'anthropomorphites' were wrong to think that God has arms and legs. Does it follow that they were wrong to think of him as physical? What do we *mean* by physical in the first place? To the Stoics, to exist and to be physical meant the same thing, because in their view a non-physical object could not do anything or have any effect on the world at all – and for them, that was the same thing as not existing. That was Tertullian's reasoning:

> How could it be, that he himself is nothing, without whom nothing was made? How could he who is empty have made things which are solid, and he who is void have made things which are full, and he who is incorporeal have made things which have body? ... For who will deny that God is a body, although 'God is a Spirit'? For Spirit has a bodily substance of its own kind, in its own form.[3]

Tertullian thus assumes that to call something incorporeal is the same thing as to call it nothing. But clearly theologians such as Origen would disagree with this premise in the first place, since they believed that God was not physical but nevertheless existed and acted upon the physical world. So what did 'physical' and 'spiritual' mean for them? It's not always obvious. One criticism that materialists sometimes make of those who believe in non-material entities is that they never seem to come up with a good description of them, or if they do, it's always made up only of negative terms. A spiritual thing (such as God) is not physical, lacks shape, colour and motion, is not confined to any location, and so on. What *is* it, then?

God Known and Unknown

The fact that it's surprisingly hard to explain precisely what it means to call something 'spiritual' as opposed to 'physical' is connected to another fundamental disagreement within Christianity about God's nature. To what degree can God be known?

A number of Christian theologians have emphasized God's knowability. Once again, Origen is a prime example. Like many Platonists, Origen believed that knowability was a perfection. If something couldn't be understood, it was in some way vague or poorly formed. Thus, God could be (in theory) perfectly known and understood. Indeed, Origen thought that God was finite, for something infinite could never be perfectly known. To a Platonist, for something to be perfect it had to be a perfect *something* – that is, a particular kind of thing. It couldn't just be vaguely 'perfect' in general. But of course, if the perfect thing were a particular kind of thing, it would equally be not any other kind of thing. On this view, then, God would be defined in a fairly narrow way as a particular kind of thing, a finite thing. Nevertheless, Origen did think that it was extremely hard to come to know God, and certainly in this life, where we are distracted by bodily things. He wrote:

Strictly speaking, God is incomprehensible, and cannot be measured. For whatever knowledge we may get of God – either by perception or reflection – we must necessarily believe that he is far better than what we perceive him to be. It is as if someone were unable to bear the sight of a spark of light, or a very dim lamp, and we wanted to make a person whose eyes could not stand a greater light than that aware of the brightness of the sun – wouldn't it be necessary to tell him that the sun's splendour is unspeakably and incalculably better and more glorious than all the light he sees? ... Our eyes often cannot look upon the nature of the light itself – that is, upon the substance of the sun – but when we see its splendour or his rays pouring in, perhaps through windows or some small openings to let the light in, we can reflect how great is the supply and source of the light of the body. So, in the same way, the works of Divine Providence and the plan of this whole world are a sort of ray, as it were, of the nature of God, compared to his real substance and being.[4]

In this view, we may not be able to understand God perfectly (or indeed very well), but we can still have quite a good idea of what he is like, perhaps by looking at the world which he created. After all, when God appeared to Moses it was in the burning bush – an epiphany of light, reflecting the fact that when you encounter God you *learn* things about him. For Origen, spiritual progression was an intellectual discipline, centred on studying the Bible. The more you studied, the more you knew, and the more you knew, the closer you were to knowing God. According to Origen, God is pure intellect, the greatest mind in the universe, and so intellectual and spiritual enlightenment are exactly the same thing. We find this 'light-centred' theology cropping up often in later writers – hardly surprising, given that John's Gospel makes frequent use of the light–dark dichotomy.

This is sometimes called a 'cataphatic' spirituality, literally 'down from above', since it is based on the idea that God reveals things about himself to human beings. In Western Christianity, cataphatic theology has probably been the most common kind. But even as Origen was setting forth his vision of God, an alternate one was developing, according to which God *can't* be known – not even in the limited way that Origen allowed. In the early years of the third century, Origen's own teacher, Clement of Alexandria, had written the following difficult but extremely influential passage:

> We abstract from the body its physical properties, taking away the dimension of depth, then that of breadth, and then that of length. For the point which remains is a unit, as it were, having position. And if we abstract position from that, there is the conception of unity. If, then, abstracting everything that belongs to bodies and to things that are called incorporeal, we cast ourselves into the greatness of Christ, and from there advance into immensity by holiness, we may reach somehow to the conception of the Almighty – knowing not what he is, but what he is not. And form and motion, or standing, or a throne, or place, or right hand or left, are not at all to be conceived as belonging to the Father of the universe, although it is so written. But what each of these means will be shown in its proper place. So the First Cause is not in space, but above both space, and time, and name, and conception.[5]

In this view, God is so far beyond the universe that we cannot apply categories drawn from the universe to him. Clement suggests that we imagine a physical object and then strip from it, in our minds, all the qualities that it has *as* a physical object; what we are left with is the notion of pure existence. In this way, the 'knowledge' we have of God is really just knowledge of what he is not, not of what he is.

Clement was a Christian, but he was greatly influenced by non-Christian philosophers and other writers, and his basic approach to this matter was increasingly common among Platonists in the second and third centuries. One of the most commonly quoted lines from Plato himself during this period was a sentence from his dialogue *Timaeus*: 'It is hard to find the maker and father of the universe and having found him, it is impossible to speak of him at all.' In fact, this single line was quoted so often it was virtually a cliché. Philosophers and theologians alike used it to support the idea that God is intrinsically unknowable; that is, he doesn't just happen to be unknown because we are not very clever. Even the most perfect created mind imaginable *could* not know God, because he transcends the universe so utterly.

In the late fourth century, the major Christian theologian Gregory of Nyssa pioneered this approach. He was the first Christian to argue that God is literally infinite. This may seem odd to many today, since God is normally described as infinite, but this was not the case in antiquity. Gregory argued that anything finite could in principle be surrounded or constrained by its opposite, but this is surely not the case with God. He also pointed out that, according to the book of Exodus, Moses did first meet God in the light of the burning bush, but when he climbed the holy mountain to receive the Law, he passed through first cloud and then darkness. This signifies that the more you learn about God, the more you realize you don't (and can't) know about him. So where Clement of Alexandria had offered a rather philosophical approach to God's unknowability, involving the analysis of concepts, Gregory described one based on experience: we know that God can't be known because that is how we experience him. Indeed, even the name 'God' (or whatever else we want to call him) doesn't really refer to God himself, if by that we mean the ultimate reality. It refers only to his actions and how he appears to us. The *real* God, the reality beyond our perceptions of him, is intrinsically barred from our understanding. In the early sixth century, an anonymous writer known as Pseudo-Dionysius expressed this idea with remarkable clarity and brevity:

> For the higher we soar in contemplation the more limited become our expressions of that which is purely intelligible; even as now, when plunging into the Darkness which is above the intellect, we pass not merely into brevity of speech, but even into absolute silence, of thoughts as well as of words.[6]

Such an approach is called 'apophatic' spirituality – literally, theology 'going out' from what we can know to what we cannot. It is also sometimes called the *via negativa* or 'the negative way', a name given it by the fifth-century pagan Platonist philosopher Proclus, who was a major influence on Pseudo-Dionysius. Pseudo-Dionysius endorsed both cataphatic and apophatic theology, but suggested that the latter was more profound and, ultimately, 'truer' than the former. This view was enormously influential in both Western and Eastern Christianity. His basic approach was incorporated into the theological systems of the greatest medieval representatives of both traditions: in the East, the fourteenth-century Gregory Palamas, and in the West, the thirteenth-century Thomas Aquinas. Palamas, for example, distinguished between God's 'essence' and his 'energies': we can know the latter but not the former. His distinction was endorsed by councils held at Constantinople in 1341 and 1351 and became central to the Orthodox understanding of God.

Yet many Christians have felt uncomfortable with this tendency. For one thing, some mystics have emphasized the unknowability of God to such an extent that they seem to have nothing left of him at all. If the word 'God' doesn't really refer to *God*, then how do we know that there is any such thing? And if there is, what exactly is it, if not what we normally think of as 'God'? Meister Eckhart, a highly influential mystic of the late thirteenth century, could write at one point that God is the fullness of being (that is, the most existent thing there is) and at another that God doesn't exist at all (that is, he has no qualities that we would normally suppose an existing thing to have). It is little wonder that Eckhart was tried for heresy within his lifetime (and remains rather controversial today): for many people, ideas such as these seemed indistinguishable from atheism pure and simple.

God Transcendent and Immanent

Thomas Aquinas is another name we shall encounter often in these pages: generally regarded as the greatest philosopher and theologian of the Middle Ages, he constructed an impressive philosophical system in which he tried to combine the Christian faith he inherited from Augustine and other earlier thinkers with secular philosophical and scientific thinking, above all that of Aristotle. His doctrine of God was a prime example of this, and it was intended to express Pseudo-Dionysius' basic view in a more rigorous way. Like others in the Aristotelian tradition, Aquinas distinguished between an object's 'essence' and its 'existence'. Something's 'essence' is simply the kind of thing that it is, its qualities. But to ask what something is – what characteristics it has – is different from asking whether it exists. You can understand the essence of something without even knowing whether it exists; for example, mathematicians can talk about the properties of a certain triangle whether or not any triangle of those proportions actually exists. And you can realize that something exists without knowing what it is, as when you glimpse a shadowy figure in the distance but cannot make out its features. According to Aquinas, the only exception to this distinction is God. In God's case, his essence is his existence. If you ask what kind of thing he is, the answer is, 'He exists' – just as God himself said to Moses, according to the story in Exodus. Aquinas points out that most things have their existence caused by something else, which is why their existence is not the same thing as their essence. But God is not caused by anything else. You therefore cannot explain his existence by referring to anything outside his essence; his existence *is* his essence.

Aquinas' doctrine sounds rather peculiar, especially to modern ears not used to talk of essences and existences. But the point is perhaps at root a rather simple one. It is that God is not an object like others – not even the greatest object. He is not a *thing* to be found in the universe. If you were to make an enormous list of every object in the universe, God would not be on the list. He transcends the universe. More than that, he is what allows the universe to exist at all. If God's essence is existence, then there is a sense in which we can say that God simply *is* existence. For something to exist is, in some way, for it to share in God's being.

There was nothing new about this basic view. Irenaeus, a major theologian of the late second century, had described God as holding the universe in the palm of his hand, and as enveloping the universe so that nothing could exist outside him. Another theologian of this period, Marcus Minucius Felix, put his view like this:

> It is said that God does not know what human beings do; and being established in heaven, he cannot see everything or know everyone. You are wrong, O man, and are deceived. For where can God be far from, when all things in heaven and earth, and those beyond the universe, are known to God and full of God? Everywhere he is not just very close to us but infused into us. So look again upon the sun: it is fixed securely in the sky, but it is diffused over all lands equally. It is present everywhere, associated and mixed with all things, its brightness never compromised. How much more is God – who made everything, and sees everything, from whom nothing can be kept secret – present in the darkness and present in our thoughts, as if in the deep darkness. Not only do we act in him, but I could almost have said that we live with him.[7]

This leads to something of a paradox. On this view, God transcends the universe to such a degree that he is not like the things in it: he belongs to a completely different category altogether. Yet, at the same time, the universe exists *in* God in some sense. This isn't meant in a crudely literal way – God is not the 'place' in which the universe is located; rather, God is, as it were, the glue that holds the universe together. That means that God is not just transcendent but 'immanent', that is, present in everything.

This understanding of the relation between God and the world was expressed perhaps most famously by Nicolas Malebranche, a seventeenth-century philosopher and Catholic priest. Malebranche stated that we perceive all things 'in God', a rather obscure comment which has been interpreted in a number of different ways. On one reading, Malebranche rather crudely believed that our sense impressions are caused not by external objects acting upon us but by God directly: thus, the things that we directly see, hear and touch are just ideas in the mind of God. On an alternative reading, Malebranche meant that our *conceptions* of objects are ideas in the mind of God. When we see something, we know what it is only because God knows what it is, and he gives us that knowledge directly. Whenever we think 'about' something, that thing is actually an idea, a definition of the thing, in God's understanding. Either way, God plays an extremely intimate role in our perception of the world around us and even in our very thought processes – for whenever we think about anything, we are really thinking about God's ideas. Malebranche also held a form of occasionalism, a doctrine which had been pioneered by medieval Muslim philosophers (most famously the eleventh-century Abu Hamid al-Ghazali), and which was not uncommon in seventeenth-century Europe. According to this view, physical objects are intrinsically inert: they never act upon each other. So when one object bumps into another and seems to move it, what really happens is that God moves the first object, makes it stop, and then moves the other one. In other words, everything that happens in the world happens because God does it directly. That even includes the movements of our bodies. God does not control our bodies as a puppeteer controls his puppets; rather, when you choose to move your arm, God reacts to your choice by moving your arm for you.

It is hard to imagine a view of God which puts him more at the centre of things than this. Of course, few people since the seventeenth century have accepted it. It seems unnecessarily complicated. If God does everything, why have material objects at all? One philosopher, George Berkeley, who became bishop of Cloyne in the eighteenth century, took it to its logical conclusion and argued that material objects don't exist at all. All that exists is God and minds. The world we see around us is composed entirely of ideas; these ideas are given to us directly by God, who does not need to use matter to remind himself what to do. God thus becomes the ultimate virtual reality computer system, and the world exists only in his thought. Strikingly, this view had been anticipated nearly a millennium and a half earlier. Origen seems to have suggested that only God and created minds really exist, and matter is simply a sort of illusion. Gregory of Nyssa said the same quite explicitly. At that time, many Platonists believed that the physical world had three causes: a creator God, a set of templates (the 'Forms') and matter. God moulded matter as the Forms directed. For Christian Platonists, the Forms existed only in God's mind. That only left matter as a sort of potential rival to God as creator of the world. Some Christians eliminated this rivalry by suggesting that God created matter at precisely the same time that he created the universe – that is, he created the universe out of nothing, the doctrine of creation *ex nihilo*. This doctrine was first suggested in the early second century by the Gnostic theologian Basilides; the first more mainstream theologians to teach it were Tatian the Syrian and Theophilus of Antioch a few decades later. But the alternative way of denying the eternity of matter was simply to deny its existence altogether, and this is what Gregory of Nyssa did. According to him, there is only God, and the world that we see around us really consists of his thoughts, shared with us.

Ideas like these seem very close to pantheism, the belief that the universe itself is divine. Sometimes people distinguish between pantheism (identification of the universe with God) and panentheism (the universe is part of God, or depends upon God in some very close way), and sometimes the word 'pantheism' is used to mean 'panentheism'. As this suggests, it is a hard view to define. In one sense, all orthodox Christians are panentheists, in the sense given above, if they believe that the universe depends upon God for its continued existence (as well as for its initial creation). Yet pantheism is difficult from a Christian viewpoint, for at least two reasons. On the one hand, it denies a true distinction between the divine and the non-divine, which has been a fundamental belief of Christians since antiquity. In the second and third centuries, some Christians seem to have thought it possible that there could exist a rather hazy zone 'between' God and the world, of the semi- or quasi-divine; thus Christ could be considered 'sort of' God. However, in the fourth century the Council of Nicaea expressly stated that Christ is wholly God, leaving (by implication) no metaphysical space for halfway houses. By the end of the fourth century, orthodox Christians believed in a God of three persons, distinct from the world, wholly divine. Pantheism seems expressly opposed to this viewpoint. The second problem is that pantheism can seem hard to distinguish from atheism. If the universe is God, then this seems little different from saying that there is no God (other than the universe). Some pantheists have been condemned as atheists; most famously, Baruch Spinoza, another major philosopher of the seventeenth century, was branded an atheist for his identification of God with nature. He was actually a monist, arguing that God is the only thing that really exists at all, and everything else is simply a sort of quality that God possesses. Several decades later, in the early eighteenth century, John Toland (the man who coined the word 'pantheist') gloomily commented that pantheists must maintain two theologies – a private, pantheistic one, and a public, 'orthodox' one. Otherwise their lives would be intolerable in a society that branded their views heretical and atheistic.

Orthodox Christianity has generally resisted the tendency towards pantheism, just as it has also resisted the tendency the other way, towards deism (the belief, fashionable in the eighteenth century, that God created the world but subsequently has had nothing to do with it). It is a difficult balancing act, since to resist one is to tend towards the other. The most successful solutions are like those of Aquinas, who explains God's immanence in terms of his transcendence. On that account, God is immanent only because he is so transcendent. This makes it impossible to focus too much on one aspect and ignore the other.

The Suffering God

This may be all very well, but some will not find it very inspiring. Whether God is immanent or transcendent, he is not a sympathetic character, existing in his own timeless bubble and immune to the problems that we face in our mortal existence. Here again, there has been great disagreement among Christians. For if that is the case, how can anyone say that Jesus – suffering and dying on the cross – was God?

The traditional, orthodox understanding is that God does not suffer – at least, not *as* God. That is, God does not normally suffer. However, Christ suffered, and Christ was God. According to the Council of Chalcedon, held in AD 451, Christ was one person, but he had two natures; that is, he was fully human and fully God at the same time. This meant that all the things that are true of human beings are true of him, and also that all the things that are true of God are true of him. That in itself opens up whole new problems and issues (does this mean that Christ was both omnipotent and limited in power?), but the important thing from our point of view is that it means that things that are normally true only of human beings can be said of God, and vice versa. Christ was God, and Christ suffered; so we can say that God suffered. Similarly, Christ was human, and Christ walked on water; so we can say that a human being walked on water.

This is known as the *communicatio idiomatum* (the 'communication of attributes'). It means that, when talking about the incarnation, it is possible to say that God suffered (and was hungry, tired and so on), in a way that has been orthodox since the fifth century.

Traditionally, Christians have not believed that God suffers intrinsically, as it were. Even on the cross, God suffers *as man*. The Council of Chalcedon was quite clear on this matter and condemned 'those who dare to assert that the deity of the Only Begotten is passible' (that is, capable of suffering). Later, Aquinas analysed the concept of suffering, and argued that it has two parts: first, the internal misery, and secondly, the external event that causes it. So there is my pain at being punched, and the punch itself. But, he argued, God cannot feel internal misery, because (being perfect) God is always perfectly blissful. And God cannot be subject to external events, because he is being itself, the source of existence for all other things. None of those things can turn around and 'attack' God. To put it another way, God is pure agent. He *does things* – he doesn't have things done *to* him. Or, to put it yet another way, suffering is a kind of change (a change for the worse). But God does not change, for he is eternal.

In part, such views can be found in the Bible. Consider the following passage, for example:

> For I the Lord do not change; therefore you, O sons of Jacob, are not consumed. From the days of your fathers you have turned aside from my statutes and have not kept them. Return to me, and I will return to you, says the Lord of hosts.
> **Malachi 3:6–7**

The idea here seems to be less of an impassible God than of a God who is always willing to forgive. He is constant, rather than immobile. And many other passages in the Old Testament portray God as changing:

> For a brief moment I forsook you, but with great compassion I will gather you. To overflowing wrath for a moment I hid my face from you, but with everlasting love I will have compassion on you, says the Lord, your Redeemer.
> **Isaiah 54:7–8**

This sounds like a God who doesn't simply change but who experiences emotions, including quite unpleasant ones. Moreover, when the God of the Old Testament suffers, he suffers with his people, just as the passage from Isaiah suggests. In the Old Testament, God and his people, Israel, are so closely linked that when Israel prospers, God is happy, and when Israel falters, God suffers. This has led many Christians in modern times to reject the 'classical' view of God as impassible. The twentieth-century theologian Charles Hartshorne was probably the best-known exponent of this idea. He argued that the classical belief that a perfect being could not suffer owed more to Greek philosophy than to the Bible, and that a study of the Bible actually suggests that God's ability to suffer with his people is one of his perfections. This is not a new idea either. Anselm of Canterbury had suggested something similar nearly a thousand years earlier, in the form of a question addressed to God himself:

But how can you be at the same time both compassionate and beyond passion? If you are beyond passion, you cannot suffer with anyone; if you cannot share suffering, your heart is not made wretched by entering into the sufferings of the wretched, which is what being compassionate is. But if you are not compassionate, where does so much consolation for those who are wretched come from?[8]

Anselm went on to reject the notion that God truly feels compassion; he suggested instead that he is compassionate in the sense that he acts *as if* he felt compassion, so from our point of view he is entirely compassionate. For Hartshorne and many other modern theologians, this is not enough. For God to be truly loving, he needs to be really able to suffer. That is what we expect of human love, after all: not necessarily to *actually* suffer, but to be open to the possibility. If Lex claims to love Lois, but there is no way even in principle that Lois could hurt Lex emotionally, we would be inclined to think that Lex doesn't love her at all. Love invariably involves opening oneself to the risk of being hurt.

Of course, to accept such a view of God means shedding more than simply the belief that God cannot suffer. If God can suffer, then God can change – so goodbye to the belief in God as timeless, another central tenet of the medieval doctrine of God, and one which goes back at least to Origen. Even more intriguingly, perhaps a suffering God is not an all-powerful one. Again, Hartshorne was happy to accept ideas such as this (one of his books, published in 1984, bore the provocative title *Omnipotence and Other Theological Mistakes*). He was influenced by the early twentieth-century philosopher A.N. Whitehead, who proposed a 'process philosophy' whereby, instead of thinking of the world as made up of 'substances' (as had previously been normal), one thinks of it as made up of 'processes'. In that view, there are no objects that endure through time; instead, everything is a changing process. As the ancient philosopher Heraclitus put it, you cannot step into the same river twice. Hartshorne therefore applied this notion to God, creating 'process theology', which thinks of God in these terms – a changing, and limited, process within a universe-wide network of processes.

Process theology was quite fashionable for a period, but after the 1970s its popularity waned (together with that of the 'process philosophy' that inspired it). Yet today, many theologians are still attracted to the idea of divine suffering. There are probably two main reasons for this. The first is that a suffering God is an ethical God – indeed, a politically involved God. One of the most important theological movements of the twentieth century was liberation theology, which holds that God is intimately identified with the poor and marginalized. He suffers with them, just as he suffered alongside the Israelites.

The other main reason comes from what is sometimes known as 'cross theology'. The idea is fairly simple: if you want to know about God, you should start with the cross, that is, the death of Jesus. That in itself may not seem especially radical from a Christian point of view. But in fact it involves a remarkable shift in understanding. The ancient Christian theologians – as well as the medieval ones – were quite happy to describe God without referring primarily to the cross. In fact, some Christians of the second century seem not to have been very interested in it at all: Theophilus of Antioch wrote a whole book defending Christianity without mentioning Jesus, while Minucius Felix actually denied that Christians worshipped a man who died as a criminal! Even for those more in line with later orthodoxy, the cross was not their starting point for talking about God. Anselm and Aquinas alike, for example, have a great deal to say about God as apart from Jesus. Only *after* they have set out who God is do they consider the remarkable fact that this God became human, suffered and died. In this traditional type of theology, one starts with the idea of God, and only then brings in the incarnation and the crucifixion.

The alternative view goes back to Martin Luther, who not only began the Protestant Reformation but bequeathed to his Protestant heirs a belief that the cross should be absolutely central to Christian belief. That is, it's not just an essential part of the religion, but the focal point around which all else revolves. On this basis, Luther reinterpreted the doctrine of the *communicatio idiomatum* that we saw earlier. In his view, we don't just say that God died on the cross; we can say that God's divinity died on the cross. What is true of Christ as man can now be considered true of him as God.

The best-known theologian to have explored this idea in recent times is probably Jürgen Moltmann, a highly influential German theologian. In *The Crucified God*, published in 1972, he argued that the cross is not simply something which happens to God; it reflects God's fundamental nature. God does not simply happen to suffer; God *is* suffering. Suffering is the most divine thing about him. God's suffering contains all the suffering contained in the universe: whenever anyone suffers, God suffers alongside them.

These views are not restricted to Protestants. The seventeenth-century French spiritual writer Louis Chardon, who was very popular in his day, though mostly forgotten now, spoke repeatedly of the suffering of God. Indeed, he apparently thought that Christ spent almost his entire life suffering – calling him 'the suffering God' – and claimed that it is through his suffering that Christ is closest to the Father. In other words, the union between the two is precisely the suffering of Christ. It is hard to see how this can be reconciled with the orthodox Catholic belief that the Father does not suffer, but Chardon seems not to have got into any trouble for it in his lifetime (he was actually a theological adviser to the Vatican). Moreover, Chardon was not a speculative theologian but a spiritual writer: his books were intended to edify and comfort the pious. He believed that the suffering of Christ, and of God, is inevitably expressed in the life of the believer also. That is, every Christian will also experience suffering and even spiritual desolation, but this is an essential part of the process of coming to have complete trust in God.

As we will see in chapter 3, ideas like this can be very valuable from a pastoral point of view. A person who is suffering may find great comfort in the belief that God suffers alongside them. To others, such a God seems simply weak. The philosopher Friedrich Nietzsche, writing in the late nineteenth century, when some ideas similar to Moltmann's were being proposed, hated the Christian view of God (which he dubbed 'monoto-theism'). In particular, he loathed the idea that God sympathizes with the weak or suffers in any way:

> The Christian conception of God – God as God of the sick, God as spider, God as spirit – is one of the most corrupt conceptions of God arrived at on earth: perhaps it even represents the low-water mark in the descending development of the God type. God degenerated to the *contradiction of life*, instead of being its transfiguration and eternal Yes! In God a declaration of hostility towards life, nature, the will to life! God the formula for every calumny of 'this world', for every lie about 'the next world'! In God nothingness deified, the will to nothingness sanctified![9]

A fair criticism? Nietzsche's hatred of Christianity was based, to a large degree, on the fact that he found it life-denying. He was convinced that the physical world represents the totality of reality, and that a life-affirming worldview (in other words, a good one) would recognize and embrace this fact. The Christian doctrine of the transcendent God, to him, was simply a personification of what he believed was the fundamental world-denying character of Christianity.

God Out There or God In Here?

Perhaps the most striking thing is that some Christians have agreed with Nietzsche's analysis – at least to some extent. Certainly

Nietzsche was right to predict that, in the twentieth century, there would be fundamental upheavals in many people's understanding of who and what God is. The seeds of these upheavals were planted in the first half of the twentieth century, and they came to fruition in the second half.

In particular, three German theologians wielded enormous influence. The first was Dietrich Bonhoeffer, who was executed by the Nazis in 1945. In his prison cell, Bonhoeffer mused upon the role of the church in the world, and the nature of its faith; he suggested that Christianity needed to engage with contemporary culture at its heart rather than skulking on the sidelines in a world of its own. He used the intriguing phrase 'religionless Christianity' to express this idea. Equally important was Rudolf Bultmann, one of the most prominent German theologians of the twentieth century, who achieved the rare distinction of pre-eminence in both biblical studies and doctrinal theology. Bultmann believed that the message of the New Testament was of enduring value, but the language and ideas in which that message was expressed were not. He argued that we have to distinguish between the message and the medium. For example, people in the first century lived in a mythological framework: they believed in angels and demons, and in a heaven above their heads as well as a hell beneath their feet. People today do not believe such things. But the gospel, preached by the first-century Christians, does not depend upon the existence of such things, even though the first Christians inevitably spoke about them. The task of theology is therefore to 'demythologize' the New Testament, to look beyond the mythological trappings and extract the real message, which can be translated into terms that modern people can understand. Bultmann believed that the language of existential philosophy provided the best way of doing this. This was a view he shared with a third major German theologian, Paul Tillich. Like the other two, Tillich clashed with the Nazis in the 1930s; he fled to the United States, where he did most of his important work. His three-part *Systematic Theology*, published between 1951 and 1963, was one of the most influential Christian books of the twentieth century. Like Bultmann, Tillich sought to express Christianity in language taken from existentialism. He argued that God himself is simply pure

Being. In this view, it is wrong to say 'God exists', since this would make God out to be just one existing thing among others. Rather, God is existence itself: that which makes possible the fact that anything exists. To many people, Tillich's version of theism seemed indistinguishable from atheism. If there is no 'thing' called God, does God exist at all? What does it even mean to say that God just 'is' existence? Yet Tillich's views could also be seen as simply a restatement of Thomas Aquinas' theology. If God's 'essence' is his 'existence', then is God really anything other than the sheer fact of existence itself?

Influenced by these German theologians, in the 1960s a number of English-speaking Christian writers took up Nietzsche's famous slogan 'God is dead' and, rather daringly, subverted it as a *Christian* claim. The most prominent of these theologians was Thomas Altizer. In his book *The Gospel of Christian Atheism*, published in 1966, Altizer argued for an extreme version of kenotic Christology. Kenotic Christology had been pioneered by the nineteenth-century Anglican theologian Charles Gore. Taking his cue from Philippians 2:7, which stated that Christ 'emptied himself' (*kenosis*), Gore had suggested that instead of the traditional belief in a Christ with two natures (one human and one divine) we think instead of a single divine nature that actually becomes human in Christ. That is, God divests himself of his divinity when he becomes incarnate. Altizer took over this idea, but made the radical suggestion that it was a permanent change. In place of one person of the Trinity becoming human, leaving the rest of God untouched, as it were, Altizer suggested that we think of the whole of God literally becoming a human being. And when that human being dies, God dies too. There is no literal resurrection or ascension; after Jesus' death, God no longer exists, because he literally died.

God *is* Jesus, proclaims the radical Christian, and by this he means that the Incarnation is a total and all-consuming act: as Spirit becomes the Word that empties the Speaker of himself, the whole reality of Spirit becomes incarnate in its opposite. Only the radical Christian witnesses to the full reality of Jesus or the Incarnate Word, because he alone responds to the totally kenotic movement

of God... A Christian proclamation of the love of God is a
proclamation that God has negated himself in becoming flesh,
his Word is now the opposite or the intrinsic otherness of his
primordial Being, and God himself has ceased to exist in his original
mode as transcendent or disincarnate Spirit: God is Jesus.[10]

Altizer presents this rather startling idea as the logical consequence
of the Christian doctrine of the incarnation. He suggests that this
doctrine, at its heart, is a repudiation of the pagan or Gnostic
disjunction between the physical and the spiritual. The notion of
Spirit as some eternal reality apart from the physical world is
fundamentally un-Christian. *That* God, the objective God who is
distinct from the world, the God of traditional Christianity, is
indeed dead: for it is an idol, a rejection of the real truth of the
incarnation. God is still very much alive – but he is alive within the
world and within us, not as an external reality somehow distinct
from the world.

Altizer's ideas drew on the 'suffering God' theology of Luther
and his successors, including Moltmann, but clearly they went one
step further. Not only did God really and truly suffer on the cross
– not only is suffering central to God's identity – but God really,
truly and irrevocably *died* on the cross. As a result, he today exists
only within ourselves, not 'out there' at all.

Another Christian writer to reach the same conclusion, though
for different reasons, is the Cambridge theologian Don Cupitt. In
his 1984 television series and book *The Sea of Faith*, Cupitt argued
that a non-realist view of God was actually the most authentically
Christian one. In his view, belief in God is not about accepting a
certain set of statements (such as 'There exists an omniscient,
omnipotent and morally perfect being') to be true; it is about living
in a certain kind of way.

In recent centuries the factual or descriptive elements of belief
have been steadily whittled away, until nothing serious is left of
them. When the purge is complete, we see that spirituality is
everything. Doctrines that used to be regarded as describing
supernatural facts are now seen as prescribing a supernatural
mode of existence. Disagreements between different religions and

philosophies of life are not disagreements about what is the case,
but disagreements about ways of constituting human existence,
disagreements about forms of consciousness and moral policies.[11]

His conclusion is simple. Religion – including Christianity – is
fundamentally about ethics. The other elements of religion, such
as doctrine, are actually reflections of this basic concern. Rather
than believing a set of propositions, and then behaving as they tell
us to do, we behave in a certain way and then construct the
propositions to reflect this. For example, it is not the case that we
behave in a loving way because we have been taught that 'God is
love'; rather, we say that 'God is love' because we believe we
should behave in a loving way. In fact, that is what the statement
means. In other words, the word 'God' does not refer to some
entity floating about in the sky. It is a symbol that reflects what we
most value:

God (and this is a definition) is the sum of our values, representing
to us their ideal unity, their claims upon us and their creative
power. Mythologically, he has been portrayed as an objective
being, because ancient thought tended to personify values in the
belief that important words must stand for things... The view that
religious belief consists in holding that a number of picturesque
propositions are descriptively true is encouraged by the
continuing grip on people's minds of a decadent and mystifying
dogmatic theology. In effect I am arguing that for the sake of
clarity it should be discarded entirely, and replaced by the
practice of religion – ethics and spirituality – and the philosophy
of religion. Then religion can become itself again, with a clear
conscience at last.[12]

In *The Sea of Faith*, Cupitt hints at a position that he would work
out more clearly in his later books, one of quite radical non-realism.
In his view, it is not only God who exists solely as a construct of
human language – so does *everything*. We live in a world made of
words, and the way that these words function is solely determined
by how we use them. So if 'God' is just a word, there is nothing
surprising about that, because so is everything else.

However one thinks of him – physical, non-physical, knowable, unknowable, objective, abstract or subjective – God will be a recurring character in this book. This is hardly surprising, of course. But the differing views that Christians hold on a whole host of questions reflect or influence their differing views of God too. It should be clear by now that there is no single Christian doctrine of God, but many different beliefs, some of which seem quite at odds with each other. Ultimately, even within Christianity, God remains the great 'I am' – otherwise indefinable.

Chapter 2

Have We Any Good Reason to Believe in God?

Writing to the church at Rome in the mid-fifties of the first century, Paul had some harsh words to say about the Gentiles – that is, pagans who did not acknowledge the God of Judaism and Christianity:

> For the wrath of God is revealed from heaven against all ungodliness and wickedness of those who by their wickedness suppress the truth. For what can be known about God is plain to them, because God has shown it to them. Ever since the creation of the world his eternal power and divine nature, invisible though they are, have been understood and seen through the things he has made. So they are without excuse; for though they knew God, they did not honour him as God or give thanks to him, but they became futile in their thinking, and their senseless minds were darkened.
> **Romans 1:18–21**

Paul's claim seems rather startling. Not only does God exist, but his existence is obvious to everybody; anyone who does not see this is not only stupid, but doomed to become even stupider. This seems even harsher than Psalm 14:1, according to which those who deny God's existence are fools.

Is Paul's claim tenable? Is it even plausible to say that God's existence can be known for certain at all, quite apart from the charge that those who deny it are idiots? Traditionally, Christians have agreed that there are good reasons to suppose that God exists, and that many of these reasons are available even to non-Christians. But they have disagreed over which arguments are the best, and how much they really prove – whether God's existence can be proved like a mathematical theorem, or whether some doubt always remains.

Can God be Proven?

The notion of 'proofs' of God's existence is quite unfashionable today, even among theists. There are two main reasons for this. The first is philosophical: a number of developments in philosophy in the nineteenth and twentieth centuries led many people to believe that one can never prove anything 'metaphysical', that is, about supposed realities beyond what we can immediately perceive. This would rule out any proof for (or against) God. The main figures holding this view were Immanuel Kant, at the end of the eighteenth century, and Ludwig Wittgenstein, in the twentieth. Kant argued that reason can 'prove' only things within the world of sense perception: when we try to go beyond this, we inevitably fall into error. In his early work, Wittgenstein argued that language itself cannot talk about anything outside our perception. On this view, even to talk about God is meaningless, although Wittgenstein believed that God and religion are still enormously important; they simply transcend language. But even before this, some philosophers felt that any attempt at argument was just unnecessary. For example, the eighteenth-century Scottish philosopher Thomas Reid claimed that belief in God is natural: we don't need to prove it any more than we need to prove the existence of the physical world around us.

The second objection to the notion of proof is theological, and stems from the conviction of many Christians that there is something almost morally wrong about trying to prove such a thing. Karl Barth, the most influential Christian theologian of the twentieth century, particularly hated any suggestion that God can be known apart from revelation. Such a claim, he argued, simply exalted the abilities of human beings compared with God. Instead, all knowledge of God must come from God himself, not from human reason:

> Note well: in the whole Bible of the Old and New Testaments not the slightest attempt is ever made to *prove* God. This attempt has always been made only outside the biblical view of God, and only where it has been forgotten with whom we have to do, when we speak of God... I don't know whether you can at once see the humour and the fragility of these proofs... In the Bible there is no such argumentation; the Bible speaks of God simply as of One who needs no proof. It speaks of a God who *proves himself* on every hand: Here am I, and since I am and live and act it is superfluous that I should be proved.[1]

This assertion touches on the relationship between reason and faith. If God cannot be argued for, can he be believed in at all? If so, how can such a belief be rational? We shall look at this issue in chapter 4.

In this chapter, however, we will look at just a few of the most common ways that Christians *have* tried to prove God's existence. For despite the arguments of Kant, Barth and others, many of these proofs are still alive and well today. Even those Christians who reject the idea that God can be proved like a mathematical theorem often insist that there are, nevertheless, good reasons for supposing that God does exist.

It is important to recognize that arguments can work in one of two ways. The first way is known as deductive proof. A deductive argument proves, beyond all doubt, that something is true. The paradigm example of deductive reasoning is mathematics: a mathematical proof cannot be doubted unless you doubt the basic axioms on which mathematics rests. So a deductive argument for God's existence aims to prove that God *must* exist. By contrast, an inductive argument aims to give good reasons to believe something. The paradigm example of inductive reasoning is science: you can't prove that (say) every water molecule is composed of two hydrogen atoms and one oxygen atom, but you can produce excellent evidence that could convince most impartial observers.

Historically, most Christians have believed it possible to prove God's existence deductively. This was almost a commonplace in the early centuries of Christianity. In the Middle Ages, there was more detailed discussion of the arguments, and different theologians disagreed over which ones really worked, but it was rarely doubted that *some* of them did. This remained the case well into the Enlightenment, until Immanuel Kant attacked not just the traditional arguments but the rationalist assumptions on which they were based. Since then, most Christians have thought that only inductive proofs of God's existence are possible. This case has been put most persuasively by the Christian philosopher Richard Swinburne, who presents versions of several of the arguments we shall look at in this chapter. He suggests that each one, taken individually, increases the probability of there being a God; and if we consider them all together then it is more probable than not that there is a God.

Nevertheless, deductive arguments remain alive and well in some quarters. In particular, the First Vatican Council of 1870 ruled that it is possible to prove God's existence deductively. Ever since, this view has been part of the official doctrine of the Catholic Church, although in practice many, if not most, Catholics today prefer inductive arguments.

So what reasons have Christians come up with for believing in God? There have been a bewildering array of them. We shall look at just a few of the most common.

The Hand of the Designer

By far the most common argument for God's existence brought forward by Christians is known, rather forbiddingly, as the teleological argument (from the Greek word for 'purpose'). At its most basic, it is a claim that the nature of the world is such that it must have been created by an intelligent designer. The argument predates Christianity itself, having its roots in Plato and Aristotle, but the early Christians embraced it enthusiastically. It can also be found in Judaism. Consider the words of the psalmist:

The heavens are telling the glory of God;
And the firmament proclaims his handiwork.
Psalm 19:1

This is the idea that seems to be hinted at in the passage from Romans with which we began the chapter. It was repeated, in various forms, by most of the leading Christian writers of the first few centuries, from Justin Martyr to Tertullian to Lactantius to Augustine.

A particularly vivid version of the argument is found in Marcus Minucius Felix, one of the first Christians to write in Latin, in around AD 200:

> What can possibly be so clear, so obvious, and so evident, when you lift your eyes to the sky, and look at the things which are below it and around you, that there is a God of supreme intelligence, who inspires, moves, nourishes, and governs the whole of nature? Look at the sky itself, how wide it is, how quickly it whirls around, both when it is lit up in the night by its stars and when it is brightened in the day by the sun, and you will know immediately how the wonderful and divine balance of the supreme governor works there. And look at the year, how it is made by the sun going round, and look at the month, and how it is made by the moon going round and increasing, decreasing, and shrinking. What shall I say about the constant changes of dark and light, how this gives us alternate work and rest? Now, a lengthier discourse about the stars must be left to the astronomers, about how they help navigation, or bring on the season for ploughing or reaping – all of which needs not only a supreme artist and perfect intelligence to create and arrange it, but also cannot be perceived and understood without the greatest intelligence and reason. What! When the order of the seasons and the harvests is so varied, doesn't it speak of its author and parent? And the spring with its flowers, the summer with its harvests, and the kind maturity of autumn, and the gathering of olives in winter, are all necessary – and this order would be not be stable without being established by the greatest intelligence… Look carefully at the sea – it is constrained by the law of its shore. Wherever there are trees, see how they are given life from the depths of the earth. Consider the ocean – it ebbs and flows with the tides. Look at the fountains – how they gush in never-ending streams! Look at the rivers – they always roll on in regular courses. Why should I speak of the well-ordered mountain peaks, the hillsides, the expanses of the plains? Why should I speak of the different kinds of protection

> that living things have against each other? Some are armed with
> horns, some with teeth, some have claws, some have stings, or can
> run fast or fly with wings. Even the beauty of our own figure speaks
> of God as its creator: the way we stand upright, with our faces
> looking up, our eyes placed on top as if a lookout, and all the other
> senses arranged as if in a citadel.[2]

Like most of the other early Christians, Minucius Felix appeals to
the *order* in the world as evidence of God. The idea seems to be that
order implies an orderer, as it were. Left to themselves, things
naturally arrange themselves chaotically; it is only when someone
organizes them that they become ordered. Just think of the
difference between dropping a set of chessmen onto a board any old
how, and carefully setting them in their correct positions. Minucius
Felix suggests that the world is like a correctly set up chessboard. In
which case, who's playing the game?

In the Middle Ages, the teleological argument became rather less
prominent, as the cosmological argument (which we will look at
next) grew in favour. But the seventeenth and eighteenth centuries
saw the teleological argument become more popular once again. The
love of order which most of the Enlightenment divines shared gave
them a natural affinity to this argument. Sometimes they took it
rather to extremes. The seventeenth-century English philosopher
Henry More once commented that 'Nature has made the *hindmost
parts* of our body which we sit upon most *fleshy*, as providing for our
Ease, and making us a natural Cushion.'[3] Although not all Christian
thinkers of this time would naturally have cited buttocks as
evidence for God's existence, most would have accepted More's
basic point that purely physical or natural processes could not
explain the fact that nature seemed so well put together. This is the
sort of thing that Voltaire satirized in his novel *Candide*, with the
unforgettable character of Dr Pangloss, who thought that noses
were excellently designed to rest one's spectacles upon.

Nevertheless, even those who rejected traditional Christianity in
favour of deism generally regarded this sort of argument as sound.
Thus we find new versions of it carefully set out by thinkers such as
Joseph Butler and, most famously, William Paley. In his *Natural
Theology* of 1802, Paley argued that, were we to find a watch lying

on a heath, we would naturally assume that it had a maker because of the fact that it is a complex mechanism that seems designed for a specific purpose. But the same is true of many things in the world, especially plants and animals; by analogy, therefore, it is reasonable to suppose that they had an intelligent designer too.

However, this was also the period when the teleological argument suffered two major attacks. The first came from the philosopher David Hume. His *Dialogues Concerning Natural Religion*, published posthumously in 1779, featured a devastating assault on this argument, particular the version defended by Butler (and Paley, even though Paley actually wrote later). Hume's main point was that the analogy on which the argument rests is flawed. That is, the argument assumes that objects with similar qualities must have similar origins. Thus, a chessboard is orderly because someone has set it up; the universe is orderly, so someone must have set that up too. But of course it is not true that two things with similar qualities must have acquired them in the same way. For example, one forest fire could have been started by lightning, whereas another could have been started by arsonists. In particular, Paley claims that because animals share qualities with machines, they must be like machines in some other, significant sense too. But Hume denies this. We know how plants and animals come into being; they are generated by other plants and animals. Perhaps the same thing is true of the universe. Perhaps it grew from a seed left from an earlier universe. Perhaps it was spun out by a monstrous spider. Even if it were created by intelligence, it might not have been the work of a single intelligence – perhaps several of them cooperated. And even if only one creator made our universe, there is no reason to identify him with the Christian God. Perhaps he was ignorant or rather slovenly (as the Gnostics believed); perhaps our universe is a sort of botch job by a beginner deity or a senile one. If you consider not just the order in the universe but also the disorder – the suffering and evil – then this might be a more reasonable conclusion.

Hume's arguments have generally been taken to be very effective. This has been especially so when they are taken in conjunction with the other major attack on the teleological argument, which came in the wake of Darwin's theory of evolution by natural selection. The early modern defenders of the teleological argument had been especially impressed by the ways in which the parts of animals' bodies seem so well designed for their purpose. Paley had commented that the existence of the eye alone pretty much proves the existence of God. But Darwin showed how it is perfectly possible for such things – and, of course, Dr Pangloss' nose or even More's buttocks – to emerge by following natural laws (in this case, the law of natural selection). Of course, some Christians today do not accept that Darwin was right. But even if Darwin were wrong – which, taking into account the body of scientific knowledge available today, seems unlikely to say the least – his work has still undermined the teleological argument. It shows that apparent design *can* arise without a governing intelligence. The fact that this is even possible (quite apart from the probable fact that it actually happens) suggests that you cannot infer the existence of a designer simply from what appears to be designed. As Hume pointed out long ago, to assume an analogy between artificial objects and natural ones is to beg the question.

The same thing applies to versions of the teleological argument like that of Minucius Felix, which appeal more to the cosmic order than to biology. Modern science seems to have come up with good explanations of how stars, planets and so on were formed. In the seventeenth century, Isaac Newton elegantly explained how the law of gravity and other physical laws keep the solar system running smoothly. He believed, however, that the system still required God to set it up in the first place. But later physicists and astronomers used the tools he provided to remove even that requirement: Laplace's theory of nebulae, for example, explained how the operation of gravity upon nebulae could result in a solar system forming naturally. When asked about the role of God, Laplace is supposed to have retorted, 'I have no need of that hypothesis.' He probably didn't really say that, but from the point of view of explaining the apparent order in the universe, it seems true.

But these scientific explanations only work because of the existence of the elegant laws of nature in the first place. How do we explain *them*? The Christian philosopher Richard Swinburne has argued that even though the order of the universe may be explicable in terms of natural laws, these orderly natural laws themselves imply a lawgiver (as it were). Although more sophisticated than the argument offered by Minucius Felix, Swinburne's argument does depend upon the same basic notion that order requires explanation; that, other things being equal, chaos is more probable than order. This may be true, but it is hard to show that it *must* be the case. Why, in the absence of God, would a chaotic universe be more probable than an orderly one? Someone might seek to answer that question by appealing to the second law of thermodynamics, a law of physics which states that things tend towards entropy (that is, chaos). This suggests that, ultimately, chaos wins out. If that is a universal law, then perhaps an orderly universe such as ours does need explanation. But why should we take the second law of thermodynamics to be a *necessary* law? Like all scientific laws, it only describes events within our universe. It doesn't follow that it is a necessary truth that things must tend towards chaos unless someone does something about it; perhaps our universe could have had entirely different laws of physics that did not include that law.

The Uncaused Cause

Even if we accept that the apparently designed features of the universe don't prove that it actually *was* designed, what about the sheer fact that there is a universe at all? Doesn't someone need to have made it? This is the basic idea behind what is known as the cosmological argument. Where the teleological argument points to features of the universe that suggest a designer, the cosmological argument points to the simple fact that the universe exists in the first place.

This argument was popular, above all, in the Middle Ages, when (as we shall see in chapter 5) the philosophy of Aristotle was very fashionable (though controversial) in western Europe, having been only recently rediscovered. Aristotle had proposed an early version of the cosmological argument, and a number of Christian writers in the late Middle Ages developed more sophisticated versions. For example, when Thomas Aquinas said there were five ways to prove God's existence, three of his five ways were actually variations of this argument (the other two were a version of the teleological argument and something like the moral argument, which we shall see shortly). The authority of Aquinas and the other medieval Aristotelian philosophers meant that the validity of this argument went virtually unchallenged until the middle of the seventeenth century. Descartes was accused by some theologians of being an atheist in disguise, simply because he rejected this argument, even though he put forward several other arguments of his own for God's existence.

At first, the medieval Christian philosophers got the cosmological argument at second hand, not from Aristotle himself but from the Muslim theologians who had rediscovered Aristotle. Abu Hamid al-Ghazali, for example, one of the greatest Muslim mystics and philosophers of the eleventh and twelfth centuries, defended what has become known as the Kalam version of the cosmological argument. This version proved less popular among Christians: Aquinas didn't like it, but his friend Bonaventure, one of the major theologians of the thirteenth century, was a significant proponent of it.

The distinctive element of this version of the argument is that it seeks to show that the universe must have had a beginning in time, and could not have always existed. If it had always existed, then an infinite amount of time would have passed. But according to Bonaventure, the very idea of an infinite amount of time is incoherent. If the beginning of history was an infinitely long time ago, then how could an infinite amount of time have passed and the present moment been reached? The whole point of an infinite amount of time is that you can never get to the end of it; but if an infinite amount of time has passed, then that is precisely what has happened. Bonaventure concluded that the world must have had a beginning in time.

Bonaventure then pointed out that anything that has a beginning in time must be caused by something other than itself. Here, his argument basically becomes much the same as Aquinas' second way of proving God. Aquinas writes:

In the physical world, we find that there is an order of efficient causes. We do not know of any case (and it is actually impossible) where something is found to be the cause of itself – for then it would exist before itself, which is impossible. Now, in causation it is not possible to keep going to infinity, because in all ordered systems of causes, the first one is the cause of the middle one, and the middle one is the cause of the last one (whether there are several middle causes or just one). Now if you take away the cause you take away the effect too. Therefore, if there is no first cause, there will be no last one, or any in the middle. But if in efficient causes you could keep going to infinity, there would be no first one – and, so, neither would there be a last one, or any in the middle. But that is plainly false. Therefore it is necessary to admit that there is a first efficient cause, and this is what everyone calls God.[4]

Forms of this argument remain very popular with Christians today. The idea is that all things that we find in the universe are caused by other things. And, of course, those things that cause other things themselves are caused by yet more things. But Aquinas says that we can't keep extending this infinitely. For example, say that Jacob is caused by Isaac (since he is his son). Isaac is caused by Abraham. We can explain why both Jacob and Isaac exist by pointing out who their parents were. But we can't keep doing this, because in this way we will never explain why there are human beings in the first place. If there is no first person in the chain, then there wouldn't be any later ones – but if the chain went back to infinity, there wouldn't be a first one. Similarly, we may say that each thing is caused by whatever caused it, but why are there things at all? There must be some first cause which set the whole thing going, as it were. And that, concludes Aquinas, is God.

This argument and its variants have been criticized on several grounds. One is that if we take seriously the principle that all things need a cause, then we ought to apply that to God as well. What caused him? Of course Christians have always denied that God's existence is caused by anything else. But if God can exist uncaused, perhaps the universe can too. Another comment that has often been made is that the argument as Aquinas presents it only deals with chains of causation within the universe. How do we know that the universe as a whole is part of such a chain? In other words, how do we know that the universe needs to be caused? It may be said that nothing can come into existence without a cause, but it's not clear that this is the case. The reason we think that everything needs a cause is that everything we have ever experienced turns out to be caused by something else. There is, as it were, an observable pattern. But we have only ever experienced one universe. We can't conclude that universes are the sort of things that need causes. Perhaps they are, or perhaps they aren't. To put it another way, an argument like this makes the error of assuming that the whole has all the properties of its parts. This is like saying that I can lift a brick; this house is entirely made of bricks; therefore I can lift this house. Similarly, it may be the case that each of the things in the universe has to have a cause, but it doesn't follow from this that the universe as a whole does. To assume that it does is rather like a goldfish in a bowl reasoning that everything it has ever encountered has been underwater, so therefore the bowl itself must be underwater too.

True by Definition

There is another, very different argument (or family of arguments) for God, which has proved a puzzle to philosophers and theologians alike. Known as the ontological argument (from the Greek word for 'being'), it something of an oddity in Christian history. It was first formulated by Anselm, archbishop of Canterbury, in the early eleventh century. Almost no one at the time seems to have agreed with it – in particular, Thomas Aquinas argued heavily against it. But it was rediscovered in the seventeenth century by Descartes, who proposed a much simpler version which enjoyed considerable popularity in some quarters. However, at the end of the eighteenth century, the argument came under devastating criticism at the hands of Immanuel Kant, possibly the greatest philosopher of modern times and a major influence on Christian theology to boot. Versions of it have been revived in recent years, although few people have been persuaded by them.

I won't say much about the argument here, partly because its best version (the original, by Anselm) is quite complex, and partly because it has usually been quite a curiosity. Most ordinary

Christians have either been unaware of the argument or have regarded it as completely false, and indeed it does seem to be a sort of philosophical conjuring trick, since it aims to prove that God exists simply by analysing the meaning of the word 'God'. Descartes' version, which is the simplest, runs like this. God is defined as a perfect being. One of the perfections is necessary existence – that is, not simply existing, but being unable *not* to exist. But if God necessarily exists, then he exists!

Kant's objection to this argument boiled down to the point that you can't conjure up real existence from theoretical existence. God only possesses his various perfections *if* he exists: thus, if God exists, he is omnipotent, for example. Similarly, if God exists, he necessarily exists. But it doesn't follow from that that he exists in the first place. Most Christians have indeed accepted the claim that God necessarily exists, but they have not drawn from this the conclusion that his existence can be proven.

The Moral Law Within

Immanuel Kant once commented:

> Two things fill the mind with ever new and increasing admiration and reverence, the more often and more steadily one reflects on them: *the starry heavens above me and the moral law within me*.[5]

To many Christians, both of these things that impressed Kant point to God. The teleological and cosmological arguments are really different ways of trying to find God in 'the starry firmament above'. And, particularly since the Enlightenment, many Christians (including Kant himself) have also sought to find God in 'the moral law within'. In chapters 9 and 10, we will consider in more detail how Christians have tried to understand the nature of morality and its relation to God. Here, we will look at the attempt to use morality as an argument for showing that God exists.

How could such an argument be formulated? As with the other main arguments for God's existence, this one takes several forms. Perhaps the best-known one today is the argument that the famous spiritual writer C.S. Lewis put forward in the 1940s, in his *Mere Christianity*. He begins with the observation that everybody believes, at heart, in an objective morality. As he puts it:

> Whenever you find a man who says he does not believe in a real Right and Wrong, you will find the same man going back on this a moment later. He may break his promise to you, but if you try breaking one to him he will be complaining 'It's not fair' before you can say Jack Robinson.[6]

Everyone, therefore, no matter what they claim, really believes in objective morality. Lewis goes on to write:

> It seems, then, that we are forced to believe in a real Right and Wrong. People may be sometimes mistaken about them, just as people sometimes get their sums wrong; but they are not a matter of mere taste and opinion any more than the multiplication table.[7]

Lewis suggests that each person knows right and wrong by their conscience, which upbraids them when they do what is wrong. He describes this as a sort of commanding voice within us, something implying a commander. He then points out that if there were a God, this is the sort of thing we might expect him to do. The conclusion is:

> I find that I do not exist on my own, that I am under a law; that somebody or something wants me to behave in a certain way... [There is] a Something which is directing the universe, and which appears in me as a law urging me to do right and making me feel responsible and uncomfortable when I do wrong.[8]

Versions of this argument are often used by Christians today, perhaps partly because of the great popularity of Lewis himself and *Mere Christianity* in particular. It's all the more striking that contemporary philosophers of religion seem mostly to ignore it, focusing instead on the older, more traditional arguments for God's existence. So it's worth making a few comments on the argument here.

A major advantage of this argument is that it appeals to something immediately apparent to everyone: our own thoughts, in particular our own consciences. There is something intrinsically attractive about such an argument, compared with one that invites us to engage in abstruse speculations about the origins of the universe. Indeed, Lewis himself points out that the only part of the universe which we can study from the inside, as it were, is *us*, and it is here that we find evidence of God.

However, the argument, at least as Lewis states it, does not really work as a proof of God's existence. One initial problem is that it isn't the case that everyone believes in an objective right and wrong. Despite Lewis' protests, there do exist people who do not believe in an objective morality – at least, not in the sort of objective morality that he seems to be thinking of. And not all such people are psychopaths: a great many philosophers reject the notion that there exist moral facts. They argue that moral language doesn't describe the world; rather, it has a more complex function. It is certainly not the case that *either* there are objective moral facts *or* one cannot legitimately use moral language, because perhaps moral language isn't descriptive in the same way that (say) scientific language is. But Lewis assumes that moral language functions in exactly the same way as any other form of descriptive language, and argues that we must indeed make this choice: either there are objective moral facts or we shouldn't be using moral language at all. And he concludes from the fact that everyone wants to use moral language that there must be objective moral facts.

Even if we ignore the concerns about how moral language works, though, it seems very problematic to move from the claim that everyone *believes* in objective morality to the claim that there really *exists* objective morality. The notion that what most people believe is probably true goes back at least to Aristotle, and as a general maxim there is no doubt something to it, but it is certainly not an infallible guide. After all, most people are not Christians, but that doesn't mean that Christianity is not true. This is the case even if we were to suppose that, as a psychological matter of fact, it was impossible not to believe in an objective morality. In the second of the passages quoted above, Lewis shifts subtly but invalidly from the claim that it's impossible not to believe in a real, objective morality to the claim that such a morality exists (and it is possible to be right or wrong about it, just as with maths). But, of course, it is possible to explain the general belief in objective morality without assuming that the belief is true. Perhaps, at an early stage of the emergence of human societies, there were societies where people didn't believe in morality, or who thought that murder was right, and so on. Such societies would inevitably die out. So it is perfectly plausible to suggest that the widespread belief in right and wrong – and the belief that murder is wrong, or helping others is right – came about because without such beliefs society would have died out. It doesn't follow from this that the beliefs in question are actually true.

Finally, even if there really is an objective right and wrong, it doesn't follow from this that there must be a God. In fact, many philosophers have argued for various means of establishing an objective morality without needing to invoke God. Kant, for example, believed that morality can be demonstrated and explained rationally without needing to bring God into the equation (although he also believed in God, and thought that God does command what is morally right; it's just that you don't need God to explain how morality works). Other philosophers have argued for the objectivity of morality as a human construct. After all, human beings create many things, which are no less real and objective just because they are human creations – why shouldn't the same be true of morality?

So Lewis' argument seems quite flawed, at least if it is intended to demonstrate God's existence to the unbeliever. Like many of the other arguments we have seen, it may have more value as an account of God's role in the world, addressed to those who already believe in God. That is, given that we believe in God, and given that we believe in morality, it may be that our belief comes from God himself.

In fact, something like this argument was suggested in the eighteenth century by the Irish preacher and philosopher Francis Hutcheson. Hutcheson is remembered as one of the major figures of 'sentimentalism', the claim that moral truths exist and we know them by a 'moral sense' that is in some way analogous to perception. Hutcheson suggests that:

> ...this very moral sense, implanted in rational agents, to approve and admire whatever actions flow from a study of the good of others, is one of the strongest evidences of goodness in the Author of nature.[9]

Hutcheson wasn't in the business of trying to prove God's existence. If he had been, his argument would have been unconvincing – for, as I have suggested, the mere possession of a 'moral sense' wouldn't prove that morality is real (only that we believe it to be real). But if one believes in God, and also accepts Hutcheson's claim that he has 'implanted' a moral sense into his creatures so they can perceive right and wrong, then this might indeed be a good act on God's part.

A weaker version of the argument is sometimes given, according to which, without belief in God, morality is impossible and society will break down. Consider, for example, this comment made in 1985 by the American politician Pat Robertson:

> When there is no vision of God, when there's no vision of God's law, when there's no vision of right and wrong, where there's no vision of ultimate reward and ultimate punishment, when there's no vision of decency, when there's no standard of values, society breaks apart and everybody does what he wants to do.[10]

However, it doesn't seem to be true that those who don't believe in God necessarily reject morality or lead immoral lives. There have, of course, been famously profligate atheists, such as John Wilmot, the notorious earl of Rochester; yet there have also been just as many perfectly moral and upstanding ones, such as David Hume. And the same can be said of Christians too. Despite the many good things achieved by Christians over the centuries, the notorious misdeeds also committed by the church mean that any attempt to appeal to belief in God as a sort of guarantee of morality is going to be problematic. And quite apart from all this, even if Robertson's statement were completely true, it wouldn't show that God must exist. All it would show is that it is expedient for everyone to believe in God. Parents may think it expedient for their children to believe in Father Christmas, because such a belief encourages them to be good, but it doesn't follow from that that he actually exists.

The Noble Testimony

Hutcheson thought that the moral sense provides evidence for God's goodness. Some other Christians have taken this idea slightly further, to suggest that human beings have a kind of innate knowledge of God, implanted in them by God, and they have access to this knowledge (even if they don't realize it) without having to bother with arguments, whether teleological, ontological or whatever.

The first major Christian writer to suggest this line of argument was Tertullian. Tertullian was (probably) a lawyer before his conversion to Christianity towards the end of the second century, and in his short essay *On the Testimony of the Soul* he addresses the reader's own soul as if it were a witness in a trial. He stresses that he is talking about the souls of ordinary people, not of the educated types who might already know the philosophical arguments for or against God, and he addresses the souls of such people like this:

> I do not call you when, formed by schools, trained in libraries, fed in Greek academies and porches, you belch out 'wisdom'. I speak to you simple, basic, uncultured and untaught, as with people who have you and nothing else – that thing of the road, the street, the workshop. I want your lack of experience… I ask of you only the things that you bring with you into people, which you know from either yourself or the person who made you – whoever he may be.[11]

Tertullian goes on to argue that, in everyday life, people talk as if God were not only real but watching. For example, people say things like 'God bless you!' or 'God willing' or 'May God judge between us.' So whatever they may profess, people really do believe in God at heart. Again, the fact that people worry about their reputations even after their death suggests that they really do know that there is life after death, whether they admit it or not. Tertullian concludes:

> These testimonies of the soul are as simple as they are true, common as they are simple, universal as they are common, natural as they are universal, divine as they are natural. I don't think they can seem frivolous or feeble to anyone who reflects on the majesty of nature, which is where the soul gets its authority. If you acknowledge the authority of the mistress, you must accept it in the disciple too. Well, nature is the mistress here, and the soul is her disciple. But everything that one has taught or the other has learned has come from God – the teacher of the teacher.[12]

Or, as he puts it elsewhere, 'O noble testimony of the naturally Christian soul!'[13]

Few Christians have defended this argument as Tertullian puts it. It seems hard to draw conclusions simply from the way people talk. As we saw in the last section, the fact that people typically believe in objective morality does not itself prove that there really is an objective morality; similarly, even if everyone talks as though there is a God, that would not prove that there really is. This is quite apart from the fact that people evidently talked about God more in Tertullian's day than they do now!

Descartes gave a version of this argument too, based not on language but on the idea of God. He pointed out that we have a concept of a perfect being. But where does this concept come from? It cannot come from ourselves, since we are not perfect, and Descartes thinks that the source of a concept must be just as great as the concept itself. He concludes:

> By the name 'God', I understand a substance infinite, eternal, immutable, independent, all-knowing, all-powerful, and by which I myself, and every other thing that exists, if any such there be, were created. But these properties are so great and excellent, that the more attentively I consider them the less I feel persuaded that the idea I have of them owes its origin to myself alone. And thus it is absolutely necessary to conclude, from all that I have before said, that God exists.[14]

Again, this argument doesn't seem to have been very popular. A fairly obvious rejoinder is that concepts don't have the same sorts of qualities as the things they are concepts of – the concept of an elephant is not heavy, for example. So the concept of a perfect being needn't itself be perfect, which means you don't have to posit a perfect source for it. John Locke, writing a few decades later, pointed out that you could simply think of the concept of yourself and then expand it, as it were, omitting your flaws and extending your good points infinitely.

In the twentieth century, the Catholic theologian Karl Rahner proposed an intriguing idea which is similar in some ways to those of Tertullian and Descartes. Rahner believed that a fundamental awareness of God is somehow basic to all human knowledge and experience. He is rather like the horizon: even when you can't see it, it is always there. It is impossible to paint a picture without a horizon whether you explicitly put it in or not. Rahner called this a 'transcendental' revelation, meaning that when you try to understand it you inevitably fail. It is a mystery, for God himself is the mystery at the heart of existence.

Proofs?

It's hard to see a real argument in the theory of Karl Rahner that we just looked at. Certainly, anyone who *doesn't* believe in God is unlikely to be convinced by the claim that they experience God all the time but they just don't know it. Yet it does, perhaps, make sense as a theological doctrine. That is, if you already believe in God, it may seem reasonable to suppose that he somehow underlies all our experience and is close to us even when we do not consciously feel him. It doesn't work as a proof for the sceptical, but it does as a doctrine for the faithful; not because the faithful have lower standards than the sceptical, but because the idea is simply being used for a different purpose.

I've suggested that all of the traditional Christian proofs for the existence of God seem to be flawed in one way or another. As Barth put it, they are marked by 'humour and fragility'. Certainly, they rarely seem to be effective in convincing people who do not believe in God that in fact he exists. This is especially so when we think of them as deductive arguments rather than inductive ones. One rare example in recent years of someone being converted to theism by arguments like these is the philosopher Anthony Flew, who spent many years arguing vigorously for atheism. In 2004, however, he commented that examination of the cosmological argument had convinced him that perhaps there really was a divine creator of the universe, although he remained equally convinced that the existence of suffering proves that any such creator cannot be perfectly good. As his case suggests, on those occasions where proofs like this do convince people, they generally don't result in anything like a religious conversion. It's more like acceptance of a scientific theory. As we shall see in chapter 4, though, there is more to religious faith than that.

So what use are these arguments? They make more sense if we interpret them in a similar way to Rahner's doctrine of transcendental revelation. For example, it may not be possible to convince a sceptic that the universe must have been created by God, or that the existence of orderly laws of nature points to an orderly lawgiver. But these are still roles that Christians traditionally assign to God. Christians can see the hand of God in the world around them, for example, even if they can't prove to others that it is there. The arguments themselves may be criticized – and indeed all seem to have quite serious flaws – but the doctrines that they express have always been central to the Christian faith.

Chapter 3

How Can Anyone Believe in God When There is So Much Suffering?

On the morning of 1 November 1755, a massive earthquake rocked the Portuguese city of Lisbon. As buildings crumbled, the city itself caught fire, and the river burst its banks and devastated what was left. Thousands of people perished in a matter of minutes, and thousands more died slowly in the rubble.

The earthquake was not just a humanitarian disaster. It was also a massive blow to the confidence of European intellectuals, who until that point had been busy congratulating each other on the fact that – thanks to the work of Galileo, Newton and others – the natural world was close to being perfectly understood. It was an even greater blow to those who had believed that this rational, comprehensible world is an expression of the orderliness and goodwill of God himself, its creator. German intellectuals, for example, were still under the sway of Christian Wolff, who had died eighteen months earlier. Wolff was greatly influenced by G.W. Leibniz, a brilliant philosopher who had devoted much time to trying to reconcile God's goodness with the existence of evil. Both Leibniz and Wolff argued that, since God is perfect and all-powerful, the world that actually *does* exist must be the best world that possibly *could* exist.

The great writer and critic Voltaire, normally known for his witty and clever attacks on religious orthodoxy, was deeply moved by the disaster and its implications for those who, like Wolff, sought to defend belief in a good God. His *Poem on the Lisbon Disaster* puts the point across forcefully:

Come, ye philosophers, who cry, 'All's well,'
And contemplate this ruin of a world.
Behold these shreds and cinders of your race,
This child and mother heaped in common wreck,
These scattered limbs beneath the marble shafts –
A hundred thousand whom the earth devours,
Who, torn and bloody, palpitating yet,
Entombed beneath their hospitable roofs,
In racking torment end their stricken lives.
To those expiring murmurs of distress,
To that appalling spectacle of woe,
Will ye reply: 'You do but illustrate
The Iron laws that chain the will of God'?
Say ye, o'er that yet quivering mass of flesh:
'God is avenged: the wage of sin is death'?...

Think ye this universe had been the worse
Without this hellish gulf in Portugal?
Are ye so sure the great eternal cause,
That knows all things, and for itself creates,
Could not have placed us in this dreary clime
Without volcanoes seething 'neath our feet?
Set you this limit to the power supreme?
Would you forbid it use its clemency?
Are not the means of the great artisan
Unlimited for shaping his designs?[1]

Voltaire's rhetorical question to Wolff and his ilk ushered in the modern discussion of what is often called 'the problem of evil'. At its most basic, the problem is simply that of reconciling the existence of a good, all-powerful God with the apparent imperfection of the world. Wolff's reasoning seems impeccable: if God truly created this world, and he is as good and powerful as his worshippers believe, then this world must be as good as it possibly could be. And yet we see people mangled beneath the rubble of an earthquake, and many other horrors besides.

Three Problems in One

In fact, although writers since Voltaire have often spoken of *the* problem of evil, there are really several distinct – though related – problems, which are not often distinguished. As we review the various Christian responses to this subject, it is useful to ask ourselves which question they are actually trying to answer. An answer may be useful when applied to one question, but less so when applied to another.

A Metaphysical Conundrum

The question that Voltaire asked was, in part, an ethical one. He wanted to know how a good God could permit such suffering. Wouldn't this be something of an immoral act on God's part? That seems a natural question in the circumstances. So it may come as something of a surprise to find that the first really sustained treatment of the nature of evil within the Christian tradition didn't focus on morality at all, but on a far more abstract question of metaphysics.

The question arose within the Neoplatonic tradition. Generally, the word 'Neoplatonism' is used to refer to the movement that began with the philosopher Plotinus in the third century AD: it was a development of the 'Middle Platonism' which had been a major philosophical movement throughout the couple of centuries preceding it. Unlike most Middle Platonists (who typically thought the world had several causes, such as God, the matter out of which he created the universe and the template after which he patterned it) Neoplatonists placed great emphasis on the divine as the sole source of all existence. Plotinus himself believed that everything that exists derives from the One, a mysterious and indescribable reality beyond reality. He also thought that existence is intrinsically good, which means that everything that exists is basically good. This view was intended, in part, to combat Gnosticism, a major movement of the time that existed partly within Christianity. Gnostics thought that the physical world was evil, having been created by some kind of malicious or flawed deity in opposition to the true God, who created spiritual things.

The Gnostics had an explanation for the existence of evil, but of course the Neoplatonists had more of a problem. If God (or the One) is the source of all existence, is he the source of evil too? It's important to note that the question is really a purely metaphysical one rather than an ethical one. It was a generally accepted principle among Platonists of whatever variety that like produces like. A fire heats us because it is hot; ice cools us because it is cold. So how could evil come from what is good? It is a speculative question, rather like someone who sees two sticks being rubbed together to create fire wondering how hot fire could come from cold sticks.

Evidence against God

The metaphysical conundrum faced by the Neoplatonists is largely of only historical interest now. In particular, the principle of 'like is caused only by like' doesn't seem so convincing – you can create fire by striking a match, so you *don't* need something hot to create heat. Far more important in modern times have been arguments which have used the existence of evil to conclude that God either cannot exist or very probably does not.

There is nothing new about such arguments. In fact, the first philosopher known to have formulated such an argument is Epicurus, who lived in the third century BC. His argument is reported by the Christian theologian Lactantius in the early fourth century AD like this:

> God, [Epicurus] says, either wishes to take away evils, and is unable to do so. Or he is able, and is unwilling to do so. Or he is neither willing nor able. Or he is both willing and able. If he is willing and is unable, he is feeble, which is not in accordance with the character of God. If he is able and unwilling, he is wicked, which is equally at variance with God. If he is neither willing nor able, he is both wicked and feeble, and therefore not God. If he is both willing and able, which is the only suitable way to describe God, then where do evils come from? And why does he not remove them?[2]

In the twentieth century, a number of philosophers made careful restatements of this argument. The idea is that the existence of suffering is actually inconsistent with the nature of God as described by Christians. If there were really an all-powerful, morally perfect being, he would not allow the suffering that we see. But the suffering exists, so an all-powerful, morally perfect being does not. In other words, the argument was presented as a deductive disproof of God's existence.

Although this view of the argument was popular for a couple of decades, by the end of the twentieth century it was generally accepted that it just does not work as a deductive argument. It is possible that an all-powerful, morally perfect being would in fact permit the suffering that we see around us – he *could* have some reason for it that we don't understand. Perhaps, in some incomprehensible way, this evil brings about a greater good. Or perhaps, in some equally incomprehensible way, God's hands are tied by some logical constraint that we don't know about. Either way, it is not inconsistent to believe in both God and evil. If Epicurus thought he could *prove* that God doesn't exist, he was making too strong a claim.

But of course the argument can be restated to be inductive rather than deductive (as we saw in the last chapter, a deductive argument aims to show that its conclusion is certainly true, but an inductive one aims to show only that its conclusion is probable). In this view, it may be true that God's existence is consistent with the existence of evil, but it is not likely. We imagine ourselves – or our audience – as otherwise uncommitted to either belief or disbelief in God. God's existence is, as it were, a sort of hypothesis. The existence of evil, it is suggested, is evidence against that hypothesis. Since one should aim to believe hypotheses on the basis of the evidence, the otherwise uncommitted inquirer would be best advised to reject the hypothesis of God's existence. As Stendhal put it in a letter to his friend and fellow atheist, the novelist Prosper Merimée, 'The only excuse for God is that he doesn't exist.'

This, then, is a philosophical matter. It is to be addressed by considering the argument and analysing just how effective it is: is evil really evidence against God? If so, how good is it? Is the evidence so compelling that the only rational course of action is to deny that God exists?

philosophically true that the world is eternal, even while it is also religiously true that the world was created.

At the other extreme were those who saw all this as dangerous innovation and felt that the church should have nothing to do with it. In the 1270s, Etienne Tempier, the bishop of Paris, condemned a total of 219 statements that he claimed were representative of the 'Averroism' of Siger. The University of Paris, where Siger taught and where his ideas seem to have been popular in some quarters, banned Aristotle's metaphysical books (although his writings on logic remained set texts). Siger himself was accused of heresy and fled to Italy, where a mad secretary is said to have stabbed him to death with a pen. The doctrine of 'double truth' that was associated with his name would be condemned at the Fifth Lateran Council in 1513, together with monopsychism, as well as the belief that the soul does not survive the body.

The most fruitful solution, however, was that of moderate theologians who felt that Aristotle was an extremely useful authority, but only inasmuch as he didn't clash with the church. This approach was pioneered by Albertus Magnus and his pupil Thomas Aquinas. In general, they thought that Aristotle was right on most purely secular matters, and his philosophy could be used profitably in explaining and understanding Christian doctrines. But on some matters – such as the eternity of the world – he was just wrong. Aristotelianism was thus a valuable tool in understanding Christianity, but it remained only a tool.

The Rise of Science

So the challenges of ancient philosophy and medieval Aristotelianism offer parallels, in some important respects, to the later challenges of science. Modern science itself developed in the early modern period, as a result of the empirical methods of investigation pioneered in the sixteenth and seventeenth centuries. People developed the idea that in order to learn things about the world one should carry out experiments. Thus Galileo, for example, performed experiments with weights to establish the laws governing falling (and overturned Aristotle's physics in the process, by showing that the Philosopher was wrong to assume that heavy objects fall more quickly than light ones).

For the most part, science did not represent much of a challenge to Christianity during this period. This may seem an odd claim, given that this was when the most notorious incident in the history of science and religion occurred: the pope's condemnation of Galileo in 1632 for his claim that the earth revolves around the sun, rather than vice versa. But this was not really the great clash between science and religion that it is often made out to be. For one thing, the vast majority of scientists agreed with the church, not with Galileo, who was also extremely prickly and tended to alienate people. Moreover, Galileo was condemned not so much for his mere belief that the earth goes round the sun as for his insistence that he could *prove* that it does. In fact, although Galileo did have evidence for his view, it was by no means conclusive. And the church, like most philosophers at the time, believed that scientific theories are only models of reality, not descriptions of how things actually are. In that view, it is not really true to say that either the earth or the sun revolves around the other. Rather, such statements serve simply to describe how things appear to us, and to predict future phenomena (such as the appearance of the night sky at a particular date). Ironically, this is the dominant view among scientists today.

The belief that the earth revolves around the sun did remain condemned by the Catholic Church for some time after Galileo's death. The idea apparently contradicted not only the received scientific wisdom but also key passages of the Bible. Psalm 19:4–6 and Ecclesiastes 1:5 speak of the movements of the sun, while in Joshua 10:12–13, God miraculously causes the sun and moon to stop moving (and not, as Martin Luther observed, the earth). But the church *did* remain open to scientific investigation, because it always retained the prerogative to interpret biblical passages in the light of generally accepted knowledge. In 1615, Robert Bellarmine, the cardinal charged with securing Galileo's obedience in the matter, wrote:

> If there were a real proof that the sun is in the centre of the universe, that the earth is in the third sphere, and that the sun does not go round the earth but the earth round the sun, then we should have to proceed with great circumspection in explaining passages

of scripture which appear to teach the contrary, and we should rather have to say that we did not understand them than declare an opinion false which has been proved to be true. But I do not think there is any such proof since none has been shown to me. To demonstrate that the appearances are saved [i.e., that the movements of the planets and other celestial bodies are better explained] by assuming the sun at the centre and the earth in the heavens is not the same thing as to demonstrate that in fact the sun is in the centre and the earth is in the heavens. I believe that the first demonstration may exist, but I have very grave doubts about the second.[5]

Later in the seventeenth century, many Catholic scientists devoted themselves to the study of astronomy, partly with the aim of showing that celestial phenomena are actually better explained by the hypothesis that the sun revolves around the earth. Giovanni Battista Riccioli, for example, made a careful study of the moon, and many of the names he gave its various features are still used today. Many Catholic scientists accepted the compromise system of Tycho Brahe, according to which the sun revolves around the earth and everything else revolves around the sun. However, by the eighteenth century, it was abundantly clear that Galileo had been right and that the sun is the centre of the solar system (the notion of *other* solar systems existing as well did not gain prominence until the nineteenth century). The work of Isaac Newton, in particular, had shown that no other model of the universe was really workable. Pope Benedict XIV therefore ended the ban on heliocentric books (that is, those that place the sun at the centre) in 1757.

So the whole Galileo affair, when put in context, doesn't really look like a clash between science and religion at all. On the contrary, once the science became clearly established, Christians were quite happy to go along with it, although not *all* of them were. Even today, there remain a few Christians who are convinced, on the basis of their interpretation of the Bible, that the sun does revolve around the earth. But they have been in a very small minority for over two centuries.

Far more serious were the clashes between science and religion in the nineteenth century. These mainly turned upon the new discoveries in geology and biology. In the late eighteenth and early nineteenth centuries, scientists such as William Smith and James Hutton developed the theory that the earth must be much older than anyone had previously thought – perhaps millions or even hundreds of millions of years old. The theory was based upon a careful study of rocks, especially the way in which rocks appeared in different strata or layers in the earth's crust. This, of course, clashed with the traditional understanding of the Bible, which implies that God created the world only a few thousand years ago. Moreover, the different strata contained fossils of strange animals, suggesting that at different times in history the world had been populated by different creatures, which would periodically die out and be replaced by new ones. Scientists disagreed over how to explain this. However, it is perhaps striking that many Christians did not see a real problem here. The British mathematician Charles Babbage wrote in 1837:

> I intreat the reader to consider well the difficulties which it is necessary to meet. 1st. The Church of England, if we may judge by the writings of those placed in authority, has hitherto considered it to have been expressly stated in the book of Genesis, that the earth was created about six thousand years ago. 2dly. Those observers and philosophers who have spent their lives in the study of Geology, have arrived at the conclusion that there exists irresistible evidence, that the date of the earth's first formation is far anterior to the epoch supposed to be assigned to it by Moses; and it is now admitted by all competent persons, that the formation even of those strata which are nearest the surface must have occupied vast periods – probably millions of years – in arriving at their present state. 3dly. Many of the most distinguished members of the Church of England now distinctly and formally admit the fact of such a lengthened existence of the earth we inhabit.[6]

Babbage suggested that, rather than creating the world as we know it in one fell swoop, God created a world with natural laws that would, over time, produce the world as we know it. This was actually the mainstream view among Christians in Europe by the 1840s. However, the debate became sharply polarized after

Charles Darwin published the *Origin of Species* in 1859. The book was so important not because it proposed the theory that species evolved from each other (an idea that had been around for decades) but because it suggested a mechanism which explained how this process occurred without any need for intelligent oversight: natural selection. Darwin's evidence was so convincing that within a few years of his book's appearance most scientists believed he was basically right. But this provided a serious challenge for many Christians. Not only did the history of life on earth (according to Darwin) seriously conflict with the same history as taught in the opening chapters of Genesis, but Darwin's model left very little room for divine intention in the creation of life as we know it. If it could all be explained by natural selection, what of God? Moreover, Darwin argued that human beings were part of the same process, and had evolved from creatures similar to apes. That seemed even more contrary to Christian doctrine, which had traditionally taught that all human beings were descended from Adam and Eve, who were created directly from God. In the Christian view, human beings originally existed in a happy and exalted state, and it was through Adam's sin that they were cast out of Eden and forced to endure all kinds of misery. This notion of an original happy state seemed quite incompatible with Darwin's claims, according to which human beings rose up from a lower state rather than fell from a higher one.

This, then, was the context in which modern attitudes to science and religion were formed. What are those attitudes?

Eternal Enemies

There is one very simple and popular model for the way that science and religion interact: the two are essentially opposed to each other. Religion is all about authority and tradition, whereas science is all about enquiry and questioning. Religion expects us to accept things on faith, whereas science asks to see evidence. Needless to say, the comparisons between the two are not generally made to the advantage of religion. Proponents of this model like to represent religion as the agent of conservatism and unthinking dogmatism, a force intrinsically opposed to free enquiry and the exercise of reason. The history of the two has always been one of antagonism, in which science invariably wins every skirmish, although not without an enormous amount of difficulty as the forces of religion refuse to acknowledge defeat. It was religion that condemned Galileo in the seventeenth century and Darwin in the nineteenth, and the ignominious retreat that religion has been forced to beat after those and other scuffles is just symptomatic of the triumph of reason over superstition.

This view goes back to the late nineteenth century, and the belief on the part of a number of influential anti-religious writers that the then contemporary row over Darwin was typical of relations between science and religion. The view was pioneered by the American John William Draper, who in 1875 published *History of the Conflict between Religion and Science*. As he put it:

> The antagonism we thus witness between Religion and Science is the continuation of a struggle that commenced when Christianity began to attain political power... The history of Science is not a mere record of isolated discoveries; it is a narrative of the conflict of two contending powers, the expansive force of the human intellect on one side, and the compression arising from traditionary faith and human interests on the other.[7]

His ideas were extended by Andrew Dickson White (who helped to found Cornell University) in his 1895 book *A History of the Warfare of Science with Theology in Christendom*. Both authors argued that a study of the history of ideas showed a simple pattern: superstitious clerics attributing all natural phenomena to the direct hand of God; brave philosophers and scientists showing that in fact natural phenomena could be explained scientifically; the clerics silencing the scientists; and the scientists being proved right and the clerics being forced to give up ground.

This is the model of science and religion that is presented by some scientists today. The most prominent scientists who preach this very polarized viewpoint include Richard Dawkins and Peter Atkins, both well-known popular science writers in the UK. Dawkins, in particular, has even gone beyond his remit as a scientist to publish books attacking both the claims and the achievements of religion from a philosophical and historical point of view. But do scientists such as these really understand religion as well as they do their respective subjects, biology and chemistry?

The first point to make here is that the traditional view of history which is often used to support this view is extremely flawed. We have already seen that the Galileo affair was not a matter of churchmen versus scientists, but a much more complex business, with scientists opposing each other and theological arguments being wielded on both sides. Another claim sometimes made in support of this view is that people in the Middle Ages thought the earth was flat – an example of uncritically accepting Old Testament descriptions of the world and suppressing the ancient philosophical belief that in fact the world was round. Only with the rise of modern science was the church forced to give ground. Again, however, this account of history is completely false. People in the Middle Ages – both educated philosophers and theologians and uneducated common people – were perfectly aware that the world is round and had no problem with the notion. The idea that they didn't was popularized by Andrew Dickson White who, on the basis of no evidence whatsoever, dismissed the statements of Aquinas and others that the earth is round as grudging admissions. But his revision of history has remained surprisingly stubborn ever since.

Moreover, a fairly cursory look at the history of both religion and science shows that the former has not always been the anti-rational force of darkness, and the latter has not always been the standard-bearer of free enquiry, that the Dawkins model would have us believe. Besides obvious counter-examples, such as the supremely rationalist Thomas Aquinas, our brief survey of Christian attitudes to ancient philosophy, to Aristotelianism and to early science suggests a far more complex situation. While some Christians have been opposed to any source of knowledge outside the church, others have been quite happy to accept it. And there are many examples of churchmen acting to *dispel* superstition rather than encourage it. For example, Augustine argued powerfully against the practice of astrology, insisting that it was completely irrational. As he put it, if our destinies are determined by the circumstances of our births, why do twins sometimes have very different careers?

Agobard of Lyon, a prominent bishop of the ninth century, devoted much of his time to debunking 'weather magicians' who claimed to be able to manipulate the rain clouds. He did this through logical arguments, rather than through appeal to the authority of the church. In antiquity, belief in witches – malevolent magic-users – was widespread, and the Roman historian Livy writes of mass executions of thousands of suspected witches in the second century BC. Such paranoia-fuelled massacres were certainly not confined to the Roman world, either. But by the early Middle Ages, most Christians refused to believe that witches existed at all, and the executions ceased for centuries. For example, after Charlemagne conquered the pagan Saxons in the late eighth century and forced them to convert to Christianity, he made the execution of a witch itself a capital offence. This provides something of a balancing context to the better-known period in early modern times when, for a couple of centuries, the churches changed their minds on the existence of magic and brought back the witch hunts.

Equally significantly, perhaps, men of science are not necessarily the dispassionate paragons of free enquiry that this model makes them out to be. For example, Galileo was condemned not simply because he contradicted the teachings of the church, but because he promulgated a theory that was deeply at odds with the accepted Aristotelian science of his day. His contemporaries were right to observe that he lacked sufficient evidence to prove his theory, but Galileo nevertheless insisted that he did. (Notably, Galileo insisted that the clincher was his theory of the tides, which he believed were caused by the sea sloshing about as the earth wheels through space – a theory which not only failed to prove heliocentrism, but was actually completely wrong in itself.) Some modern Christian writers on this subject distinguish between science (a legitimate discipline) and 'scientism' (something not legitimate), and argue that conflict happens only between religion and scientism. What, then, is scientism? The British theologian and scientist Donald MacKay argues that science is a matter of constructing hypotheses, examining evidence (in part, from experiments) and accepting, rejecting or modifying the hypotheses in light of the evidence. It is always open-ended, meaning that no hypothesis is ever final: there could always be some experiment that will show it to be false. But scientism, in his view, occurs when scientists take their hypotheses to be definitive claims, and then use them to attack religious views. As a brain physiologist, he uses the example of scientists who construct the hypothesis that all mental functions are caused by (or even identical with) physical events in the brain. This is science; but some then go further and not only treat the hypothesis as definitive, but use it as a weapon against those who disagree. Thus, those who think (on religious grounds) that there is more to the mind than brain processes alone are branded necessarily wrong, because they disagree with the hypothesis.

The analysis given here of science is a generally accepted one. Most scientists agree that all scientific claims are, as it were, works in progress. In theory, any scientific theory can be overturned by subsequent discoveries – and, in practice, many have been overturned in this way, or at least substantially modified. Theories about the structure of atoms current in the nineteenth century, for example, have been replaced by quite different ones today. Of course, many scientific theories (such as the theory of evolution, or the theory that the earth revolves around the sun) are supported by such massive evidence that it would require pretty spectacular new finds to overturn them. But even theories such as these are open to endless tinkering. Einstein's theories of relativity, for example, suggest that it's not really true to say that either the sun or the earth revolves around the other – it depends on your viewpoint. And Darwin's theory of evolution by natural selection has been refined by subsequent scientists to such an extent that it is common now to talk of a 'neo-Darwinian synthesis' rather than Darwinism plain and simple.

In this model, scientists certainly do overstep the mark when they treat their theories as definitive and ridicule those who do not accept them. Still, that doesn't mean that they are allowed no criticism at all. If someone insists that the sun revolves around the earth, a scientist could legitimately point out that there now exists such a vast body of evidence against this claim that it cannot really be rationally defended – unless, of course, the geocentrist has access to some incredible new evidence that has eluded everyone else. But a debate between a geocentrist and a heliocentrist is really a scientific debate. It is only when one participant brings in religion that it can become a battle between science and religion. Could it be, then, that the two are simply distinct in subject matter? This is a second view of the relationship between science and religion that has proved very popular in recent years.

The Two Spheres

In this view, science and religion do not actually clash at all, and never can, because they are about totally different things.

The claim rests on a distinction which is very common in modern philosophy: that between a statement of fact and a statement of value. A statement of fact is a claim about the world, such as 'The vase is on the table.' A statement like this is either true or false. By contrast, consider a statement like 'The vase is beautiful.' Is this true or false? According to a commonly accepted point of view, it is neither, because a statement like this is not making a claim about the world at all. We are sometimes fooled into thinking that it is, because it has a similar grammatical form to a statement of fact. But actually what a statement like this does is to express a *value*, one that is held by the speaker. We could replace it with something like 'Vase! Oooooh!' (or whatever sound you make when you see something beautiful) without any loss of meaning.

We can put the difference another way. If we are uncertain whether the vase is on the table or not, a fairly simple investigation will generally resolve the matter. But if we doubt whether the vase is beautiful, it may be that no amount of investigation will help. The vase's beauty is not a quality that it really possesses in the same way that it possesses the quality of being on the table. And if one person says that it is beautiful and another disagrees, there may be no way to determine who is right. Neither is right, or perhaps both are, because they are only expressing their own reactions to the vase; they are not making an objective claim about it. Beauty, in fact, exists only in the eye of the beholder.

This distinction between statements of fact and statements of value is fairly basic and easy to understand. And it also makes sense to apply it to science and religion. Of all human disciplines, science is the one most obviously concerned with fact. Scientists try to find out objective facts about the world and set them forth dispassionately. And religion, it is argued, is to do with value. Religion is all about loving your neighbour, doing what is right and valuing God and the world.

If this is true, then it means – very conveniently – that science and religion can never collide, provided that they each stick to their own sphere. Science describes the world, and religion tells us how to react to it. Conflict occurs when they forget their proper limitations. For example, Galileo got into trouble for claiming that the earth revolves around the sun. The Inquisition forced him to recant the theory, but in so doing they were overstepping their proper authority as guardians of religion. It is no more religion's place to judge cosmological theories than it is science's place to tell right from wrong. When religion realized this, and surrendered the issue to the scientists, the arguments stopped and everyone was much happier.

This understanding of science and religion is a very neat one. Immanuel Kant is sometimes attributed with its first formulation, with his claim that, when we are dealing with questions about the world that we see and touch around us, reason reigns supreme, but beyond that we can know nothing and must rely on faith. In fact it goes back even further, at least to the sixteenth-century philosopher and theoretician of science Francis Bacon. He argued that revelation and scientific investigation are completely different methods of knowing truth: it would be entirely inappropriate to mix them. It was a relatively short step from this view to the stronger claim that science and revelation deal with entirely different *kinds* of truth. This step was made by the Jansenists, a seventeenth-century Catholic movement of mostly French theologians. Their most famous spokesman, Antoine Arnauld, argued powerfully that matters of 'natural' fact are outside the province of religion. For example, he agreed that the pope has the power to judge on matters of 'religious' truth, such as matters of grace and free will. But he insisted that the pope cannot judge on matters of 'non-religious' truth, such as whether a certain author is guilty of making heretical statements. The pope can judge only that certain statements would be heretical if anyone made them. It has to be said that Arnauld wasn't completely consistent on this matter; he later used his connections with the Vatican to have the works of another French Catholic philosopher, Nicolas Malebranche, banned.

Arnauld believed that religion deals with *factual* claims, but these are a different sort of factual claims from those addressed by science. For example, it is a scientific factual claim to say that the earth goes round the sun; it is a theological factual claim to say that God gives us free will. Scientific investigation tackles the former and revelation (and religious authority) the latter. Kant, by contrast, thought that religion doesn't deal with factual claims at all; its province is values, which aren't really factual in any sense. Nevertheless, both positions draw a strict line between the province of religion and the province of science, and suggest that as long as everyone keeps to their own territory, as it were, all should be well.

This general position appeals to theologians who have a primarily ethical understanding of the nature of religion. It has also been defended by scientists, the most prominent being Stephen Jay Gould, the famous American palaeontologist and popular science writer. Although largely agnostic, Gould adopted quite a positive attitude to religion, and argued passionately that science and religion represent two totally different, but complementary, areas of human endeavour. His point was that both fields need to recognize their strengths and weaknesses:

The *lack of conflict* between science and religion arises from a *lack of overlap* between their respective domains of professional expertise – science in the empirical constitution of the universe, and religion in the search for proper ethical values and the spiritual meaning of our lives. The attainment of wisdom in a full life requires extensive attention to both domains – for a great book tells us both that the truth can make us free, and that we will live in optimal harmony with our fellows when we learn to do justly, love mercy, and walk humbly.[8]

But is this a realistic description of science and religion? For one thing, even if this is how they should behave, it certainly isn't how they actually do behave. As a matter of fact, science and religion have clashed ever since the pre-Socratic philosophers claimed that the moon was made of earth; and it seems highly likely that they will continue to do so for ever. And that is because, as a matter of fact, science and religion *do* conflict, both in particular claims and in their general outlook.

Consider, for example, Christian understandings of human nature. According to Augustine, human beings were originally created in a state of happiness, but through the misuse of free will fell into the unfortunate state of sin that we exist in today. According to science, on the other hand, human beings have never existed in any better state; on the contrary, we have developed from lower creatures. This is, in part, a disagreement over value, just like two people who disagree over whether a painting is beautiful or not; the scientist and the theologian evaluate human beings differently. But clearly it's also a disagreement over facts. The scientist and the (Augustinian) theologian disagree about fairly important factual claims about the history of humanity.

A Matter of Attitude

Examples such as the conflict between human nature according to Darwin and human nature according to Augustine suggest that, sometimes, religious people and scientists do say things that contradict each other. But as I've suggested above, such conflicts generally occur within the domain of science: they are disagreements about matters of fact which are (at least in theory, though often not in practice) able to be settled by scientific investigation. What makes one view 'religious' is that it is motivated by religious concerns. An example might be the belief of Mormons that, centuries before Christ, there were two major waves of migration from the Holy Land to North America. Mormons believe this for religious reasons (it is taught by the Book of Mormon). But the belief itself is about history: it is a claim that a specific event occurred at a specific time. And as such, it is subject to the usual methods of scrutiny by which historians evaluate such claims. In this case, most historians and archaeologists reject the claim: the historical evidence does not seem to support it. Similarly, whenever people make claims about the world based on religious faith, the claims are usually scientific in nature if not in inspiration, and that means they are subject to scientific inquiry just like any other scientific claims.

If this is plausible, then perhaps the truth of the matter lies somewhere between the 'eternal enemies' model and the 'different spheres' one. Science and religion mostly don't clash, because they talk about different things; but sometimes they do talk about the same things, and sometimes when they do, they disagree. That's not necessarily a matter of scientists or theologians overstepping the bounds of their disciplines and presuming to pronounce on matters they don't understand (as proponents of the 'different spheres' model argue). Sometimes, scientific or quasi-scientific claims do seem to be entailed by theological ones.

However, where science and religion do clash it seems often to be a result not simply of contradictory beliefs but of contradictory *attitudes* on the part of those who disagree. One of the most fundamental notions of Christianity – as well as many other religions – is that the universe is essentially teleological. That is, it has a purpose. In this view, human beings are not mere products of random processes; their existence is, as it were, intended. In Christianity, of course, this basic conviction is expressed in the notion of God, who created the universe with a purpose and has a plan for its future. This teleological understanding does not conflict with science if we understand science in a limited way as the examination of patterns in nature, and the proposal and testing of hypotheses about those patterns. The patterns themselves are not teleological: they have no intrinsic intent. For example, one such pattern is the fact that physical objects attract each other to a degree inversely proportional to the square of the distance between them (one of the laws of gravitation set out by Isaac Newton). But, of course, objects do not, as a rule, *want* to attract each other in this way; the earth does not revolve around the sun because it likes to travel in an ellipse. Similarly, the law of natural selection states that species tend to evolve to fit their environments, but that does not mean that species evolve on purpose, or that individual organisms 'want' to evolve. There is no sense of purpose inherent in these laws themselves: they are non-teleological. But it does not follow from this that the laws of nature could not exist for teleological purposes. Perhaps the inverse square law exists because God decided that that was how gravitation was going to work, and he had some good reason for it. The law of evolution by natural selection could have been created by a God who chose to bring about complex organisms in this way rather than by creating them himself, directly. Evolution is blind, but the *existence* of the law of evolution need not be. Science, as science, is silent on that subject.

This is not to say that scientists themselves are silent on the subject. On the contrary, some of the scientists we have already mentioned infer from the non-teleological nature of natural laws that there is no teleology in the universe at all. Nature is uncaring; therefore the universe as a whole is uncaring. Many Christians, though, have argued that such an inference is invalid. A hammer does not intend to hit a nail, but it can still be designed and used for such a purpose; similarly, the laws of nature are uncaring, but God could still have designed them for his own purposes. The British theologian and scientist Arthur Peacocke, for example, has argued at length that not only do the laws of evolution serve God's purposes, but that understanding these laws helps us to grasp a more profound appreciation of God himself. Through evolution, God is always creating. Indeed, Peacocke argues that the findings of modern science represent a new opportunity for Christians to rethink their faith. For example, instead of thinking of Christ restoring a fallen humanity, we could instead think of Christ as bringing humanity to a new and previously unattainable level of evolution. Such an approach is controversial in many quarters (does it mean that the authority of the priest is now replaced by the authority of the scientist?). However, it does seem that a constructive engagement with science, rather than a reactionary hostility towards it, is the most fruitful one for Christianity. That is the lesson of the earlier clashes between sacred and profane knowledge that we looked at in this chapter, such as the rise of Aristotelianism. Where science and religion seem to conflict, it is worth Christians (and scientists) taking the time to consider carefully whether they really do. And where they really do is where the difficult choices must be made: to what extent should Christians be prepared to criticize or modify their own traditions, and to what extent should those traditions be held sacred?

Changing Times, Changing Doctrines

That is a question that goes beyond the issue of science and religion, and one to which different Christians have very different answers. The question really comes down to this: what is Christianity *about*? What parts of their faith can – or should – Christians be prepared to modify in the face of new information from science or other disciplines? For the most part, Christians have only addressed this problem explicitly in the last couple of centuries, but it has become one of the most important questions in modern theology, and one which often lurks beneath the surface of debates that seem to be about quite different matters. Anthony Freeman, an Anglican priest well known for his liberal theological views, has written:

> There is one way of looking at doctrinal debate which sees
> Christian Truth as a package of given doctrines which are passed
> on from one generation to the next like a precious family
> heirloom... In the same way we prove our orthodoxy and our direct
> line of descent from the first Christians by continuing to hold and
> proclaim 'the faith once for all delivered to the saints'... I offer you
> an alternative and I believe more accurate model of doctrinal
> development. The tradition does not give us the answers, in the
> sense of prepackaged solutions to doctrinal questions which are
> passed down from one generation to another. It gives us the
> vocabulary to frame the questions. It is the distinctive language and
> key paradigms and stories which are passed down, not a definitive
> understanding of them. In other words, to sustain its claim to be
> authentically Christian, theology must centre on the person of
> Jesus Christ; it must find a place for the concept of God; it must
> carry a message of good news and some guidance to the living of a
> fulfilled human life. It will speak of sin and grace and salvation.
> What it does not have to do is to accept the solutions or the
> boundaries proposed by earlier centuries. Nicea, Constantinople,
> Chalcedon: they are all provisional statements in the doctrinal
> pilgrimage. They are temporary resting places, as the oasis of
> Kadesh was for the ancient Israelites; they are not the Promised
> Land itself.[9]

The 'heirloom' view of Christianity which Freeman rejects was defended most vigorously by the seventeenth-century bishop of Meaux and leading Catholic theologian Jacques Bossuet. Bossuet believed that novelty was always the mark of heresy, and the truth of Catholic teaching was guaranteed by the fact that it had never changed. Certainly there were times when the church apparently began to teach a new doctrine, but in fact it was only making explicit what had been believed implicitly before. For example, when, in the third or fourth centuries, the church began teaching the perpetuity of Mary's virginity, it was only drawing the logical conclusion of earlier teaching on Jesus' mother. And Bossuet completely rejected the views of the scholar Dionysius Petavius, who argued that the doctrines of the church had, in fact, changed over the centuries, and that orthodoxy had not been an unvarying constant.

In the nineteenth century, a sort of compromise theory was propounded by John Henry Newman. In his 1845 *Essay on the Development of Christian Doctrine*, he argued that doctrines can develop and grow just as organisms do. The oak tree is very different from the acorn, but it is, in a sense, contained within it. Newman distinguished between legitimate development and illegitimate deterioration, and provided tests by which to tell whether a change in doctrine was one or the other. His German contemporary, Friedrich Schleiermacher, offered a different model: in his account, a doctrine is simply an expression in words of an internal experience (or 'feeling'). Words may change, although feelings remain constant. The way that Christians talk today may be quite different from how they talked a thousand years ago, but it does not follow that the essential Christian experience has changed. In this view, there is nothing sacrosanct about the traditional formulations of doctrine.

Variations of Schleiermacher's view have been popular throughout the past century. The Catholic theologian Karl Rahner offered an interesting analogy of a young man, caught in the throes of first love, who tries to express how he feels in letters to his beloved. As he writes letter after letter, he comes to express himself differently, because he becomes more practised. He becomes more articulate, but his basic feeling does not change, even though he may learn to think of it in different words. However, Rahner's account, like Newman's, doesn't take into account external agents of change. Historically, doctrines haven't changed solely because of their own internal logic; they have also been affected by changes in the intellectual climate, such as the advances in philosophical or scientific knowledge we have looked at in this chapter. So some Christians have argued that the task of theology is not simply to find new words to express an old faith: it is to find new words to express that old faith to a new generation, one that does not think as the old generation did. The best-known advocate of this programme in the twentieth century was Rudolf Bultmann, who called for the 'demythologization' of the New Testament – that is, the rejection of its 'mythological' worldview and the restatement of its basic ideas in modern terms.

But other Christians have been suspicious of the enterprise. How can one distinguish between the essential message and the discardable expression? One person might view a particular story from the New Testament as myth while another person views it as the most essential part. So here again we see a diversity of different viewpoints among Christians, and ones which are not easy to reconcile with each other. The way in which different Christians approach this problem will be a major influence on the way in which they approach the challenges of modern science.

Chapter 6

Is Freedom Just an Illusion?

Freedom seems to be one of the buzzwords of the modern age. It is invoked in everything from international politics to the marketing of household appliances to computer games. Songs and albums using the word as their title have been recorded by Paul McCartney, George Michael and Jimi Hendrix, among many others. It seems that freedom is something that everyone wants, and which everyone agrees is a good thing. But what is it? And what use is it?

The notion of freedom has been central to both philosophy and theology since antiquity. In particular, Christians have regarded it as highly significant for a number of reasons. In the middle of the second century, Justin Martyr, one of the earliest Christian theologians, wrote:

> We do not believe that people do what they do, or suffer what they suffer, because of fate; but that each person does what is right or sins by choice... since, in the beginning, God made the races of angels and human beings with free will, they will justly suffer in eternal fire punishment for whatever sins they have committed. And all creatures are like this, able to do what is wrong and what is right. For no one would ever deserve praise if they did not have the ability to do both.[1]

In the first few centuries of the church, most Christians shared this view. Human beings must have free will, for without free will, morality would be meaningless: we must have real responsibility for what we do, or God could not justly judge us for it. The belief in free will, as well as the argument for it, was taken from the Platonists, who also insisted upon the importance of free will, in opposition to the Stoics, who thought that everything happens necessarily by fate.

Most Christians since have agreed with Justin. Not only does free will seem essential if God is to judge people justly, but it is essential to the 'free will defence' that we saw in chapter 3. According to that argument, one of the primary causes of suffering in the world is the misuse of creatures' free will. Clearly, if this argument is to succeed, human beings must have free will.

Two Kinds of Freedom

In Justin's day, people did not generally specify precisely what they meant by 'free will'. But in fact, the term is rather ambiguous. Ever since early modern times, it has been usual to distinguish between two senses of 'free will'.

The first is sometimes called 'contra-causal' freedom. The idea here is that an act is free if it is not determined. The fourteenth-century theologian John Duns Scotus taught this idea particularly strongly. He insisted that a free act is one that is caused solely by the will of a creature or of God; and this act of the will that causes the free act is itself uncaused. What does this mean? If an event is determined, that means that, given the preceding state of affairs, it cannot fail to occur. To put it another way: if X determines Y, then if X occurs, Y must occur too. Those who believe in determinism believe that all events are determined (including human actions). But according to Scotus – and many others – human choices are not determined. They could go either way, as it were, even right up to the last moment.

One problem with contra-causal freedom is that it seems to imply that human choices are just random. Even if an uncaused event is possible, isn't it just a random event? But of course it would be even more discomfiting to think that human choices are random than it is to think they are determined. Somehow, the believer in contra-causal freedom must describe how a choice can be neither determined nor random.

Many people – Christian and otherwise – consider the notion of contra-causal freedom to be simply incoherent. Even if it makes sense, there is the problem that it is hard to see what difference it would make. Is there any way to tell if we have contra-causal freedom? Assuming that we do have it, what effect would it have on our lives if we didn't – and vice versa? The notion seems to be purely metaphysical, in which case it seems impossible to know whether it is true or not.

However, there is a second sense of 'free will' available, often called 'compatibilist' freedom. According to this view, a person acts freely if they determine themselves. So a prisoner who cannot leave his cell lacks this freedom. Similarly, a prisoner being frog-marched from his cell lacks this freedom. Both prisoners' actions are determined by outside forces. But a person who chooses to go for a walk and then does so does have this freedom. The idea is that one's choices are determined, but they may be determined by, for example, our beliefs and desires. If our choice is determined by our own desires, our choice is free. If it is determined by something external to us, then to that extent it is not free. In this view, freedom is a matter of degree. Most of our choices are partly determined by things over which we have no control (I cannot choose to levitate, for example), but to the extent that they are determined by ourselves, they are free. This conception of freedom seems to have been developed in antiquity by the Stoics, who were strict determinists. In their view, everything that happens – including everything that we do – is fated from all eternity. Yet we can be free, if our acts are determined *by ourselves*.

One of the strongest Christian proponents of this understanding of freedom was the great Reformer John Calvin. Calvin believed that freedom was a matter of having a purified will, so that one would will only what was right. This is a process that begins when someone turns to Christ: God's grace begins to transform the believer's will, so that eventually he will desire only what is good. So human beings are always completely determined (or, to put it theologically, predestined) to do what they do, but God's grace allows them to desire what is right and to achieve it.

But what of the ancient argument of Justin and others that without contra-causal freedom there is no justice? How can we hold people responsible for their actions if they could not have done otherwise? Calvin gives this argument short shrift.

> I deny... that sin should be any less someone's fault because it is
> necessary... If anyone will argue with God, and try to avoid his
> judgment by pretending that he couldn't have done otherwise,
> the answer we have given is enough – that it is not because of
> creation, but because of the corruption of nature, that man has
> become the slave of sin and can will nothing but evil. For where
> does that inability come from, which the wicked are so quick to use
> as an excuse, except from the fact that Adam chose to subject
> himself to the tyranny of the devil?... With regard to punishment,
> I answer that it is properly inflicted on those who are guilty. What
> difference does it make whether you sin with a free or an enslaved
> judgment, provided that you sin voluntarily – especially when man
> is shown to be a sinner because he is under the bondage of sin?[2]

In other words, Calvin argues that what makes us guilty of our sin
is not the supposed fact that we were free not to do it. What
difference would that make? We are guilty of our sin if it was what
we *willed* to do. And, similarly, we deserve praise for a good act if it
was what we wanted to do. This is perfectly compatible with our will
being determined. Suppose God were to implant in me the desire
and the ability to perform a good act, and I went off and did it. The
fact that my desire came from God would not mean that I wouldn't
deserve praise. On the contrary, I would deserve praise, because I
intended to do a good thing.

Compatibilist freedom, of the kind defended by Calvin, is
called this because it is compatible with determinism. Contra-
causal freedom, by definition, is incompatible with determinism.
Although the early Christians did not define their terms in this
way, it seems that when they spoke of free will they were thinking
of contra-causal free will, because they endorsed it in explicit
opposition to the Stoics. But Augustine understood the difference
between the two views, and actually argued for both. He believed
that Adam – before sinning – had contra-causal free will. After the
fall, human beings lost this kind of freedom, and are now
determined to sin. But in heaven, human beings will have
compatibilist freedom: they will be entirely self-determined, but
their wills will desire only good. So everyone will freely (in that
sense) choose what is good.

Ever since Augustine, Christian thinkers have struggled with the dual conceptions of freedom. It is contra-causal freedom that causes the most problems. Apart from Calvin and those in his tradition, most Christians have typically wanted to affirm that this kind of freedom exists, on the grounds that it is essential for morality and justice. Indeed, Calvin's conception of free will was condemned by Popes Innocent X and Alexander VII in the 1650s; from a Catholic point of view, if we do not have contra-causal freedom, we do not have freedom at all.

The notion of contra-causal freedom is often relied upon by those Christians who use the free will defence (which we saw in chapter 3) in response to the problem of evil. It should be clear that *only* contra-causal freedom will work as part of this response. Compatibilist free will won't do. The reason is that we could have compatibilist free will, and God could *still* have set up the world to ensure that we only want what is good. Having compatibilist free will means that we can do what we want, and that is compatible with God determining that we want only what is right in the first place.

One of the problems with contra-causal free will, at least when used as part of the free will defence, is that it needs to be extremely good or desirable. The claim is that God grants contra-causal free will, even in the knowledge that creatures endowed with it will certainly (or very probably) misuse it, because it is better to have creatures with contra-causal free will than without it. But why is this? Those who use the free will defence typically assume that it is, without really going into details. We are told, for example, that God doesn't want to create mere robots. But that is a false dichotomy – a creature without contra-causal free will needn't be a robot. Indeed, many people do not believe that contra-causal free will exists at all, but that doesn't mean that these people think we are all robots.

So the free will defence theorist does need to show, not only that contra-causal free will actually exists (which would be hard to start with), but that it is intrinsically exceptionally desirable. This is not to say that these things can't be done, but the task may be harder than it first appears.

Apart from these problems that form part of the notion of free will itself, Christians have had to deal with further difficulties of reconciling free will with other Christian doctrines. Again, these issues concern contra-causal free will, not compatibilist free will. As we shall see, they have persuaded many that contra-causal free will not only doesn't exist but is incompatible with Christianity.

Free Will and Divine Knowledge

One of the major problems with freedom, from a Christian point of view, is how to reconcile free will with the claim that God knows everything. The Old Testament presents God as knowing even people's inmost thoughts:

O Lord, you have searched me and known me.
You know when I sit down and when I rise up;
you discern my thoughts from far away.
You search out my path and my lying down,
and are acquainted with all my ways.
Even before a word is on my tongue,
O Lord, you know it completely.
Psalm 139:1–4

Given this, can people really be free? Augustine was the first to put the problem in its baldest form:

I have a deep desire to know how it can be that God knows all things beforehand and that, nevertheless, we do not sin by necessity. Whoever says that anything can happen otherwise than as God has foreknown it, is trying to destroy the divine foreknowledge with the most unfeeling impiety... But I say this. Since God foreknew that man would sin, that which God foreknew must necessarily come to pass. How then is the will free when there is apparently this unavoidable necessity?[3]

Can we answer Augustine's question? It will help if we set out this argument more clearly. Imagine that I wake up on Saturday morning and decide to propose to my girlfriend:

1. God knows all facts.
2. Therefore, God knows on Friday that on Saturday I will choose to propose.
3. Necessarily, what God knows is true (because God cannot be mistaken).
4. Therefore, I necessarily choose to propose on Saturday.
5. Anything that I do necessarily, I do not do freely.
6. Therefore, my choice to propose is not made freely.

It sounds compelling, but in fact this argument is invalid. With his usual shrewdness, Thomas Aquinas pointed out where it goes wrong. It is true to say that, necessarily, what God knows will happen, will happen. But it does not follow from this that what God knows will necessarily happen. That is, the necessity applies to the whole sentence 'If God knows it, it will happen', not to the 'it will happen' part.

Three centuries later, Martin Luther rubbished this response as a 'figment'. He pointed out that even though the free action does not occur by strict necessity, it still must occur if God has foreseen it. That is, there are really two senses of 'necessary'. In one sense, a necessary event is one that could not have happened otherwise. In the other sense, a necessary event is one that cannot be altered. Now Aquinas is right to say that past events are not necessary in the first sense, but all the same, they are necessary in the second. For example, say I propose to my girlfriend on Saturday, and it is now Sunday. My proposal was not necessary in the first sense (I might have chickened out at the last minute), but from my point of view on Sunday, it is necessary in the second sense (even if I have cold feet now, I can't undo what I have done). Luther points out that God's (past) foreknowledge of a (future) free act is necessary in the second sense, just like all things in the past. But the important part is that that past foreknowledge is *about* a future event. Because the foreknowledge is infallible, it means that the future event which is known must have the same sort of necessity as the foreknowledge itself. So God foreknows on Friday what I do on Saturday. Since it is now Saturday morning, God's foreknowledge has the necessity of past events. But because it is *fore*knowledge, that necessity extends to the future event which is the subject of the knowledge.

Therefore, my future (supposedly free) act is just as necessary as God's past knowledge.

Luther concluded from this that human beings simply have no free will at all:

If God foreknew that Judas would be a traitor, then Judas necessarily became a traitor, and it was not in Judas' power – or that of any creature – to alter this, or to change his will from that which God has foreseen... If God is not deceived in what he foreknows, then the things that he foreknows must necessarily come to pass. Otherwise, who could believe his promises, and who would fear his warnings, if what he promised or warned did not necessarily happen?[4]

One problem with this conclusion is that it doesn't address the issue of *God's* free will. The issue, as we have formulated it so far, refers only to human free will, and how to reconcile human free acts with God's foreknowledge. But what about God's own free acts? They are equally hard to reconcile with his foreknowledge. Would Luther's solution work here? Traditionally, God has been conceived as possessing perfect freedom. It thus seems more problematic simply to deny that God has free will than it is to deny that human beings do.

Many Christians have responded to the whole issue with a simple move: they deny that God has 'foreknowledge' at all. The reason is that God is outside time. The Bible describes God as 'eternal' (Malachi 3:6, John 8:58, James 1:17), but it is not clear precisely what this means. So theologians sometimes contrast two different understandings of God: God as *everlasting* and God as *timeless*. The view of God as everlasting suggests that he has always existed, and he will always exist. He has, as it were, a never-ending (and never-beginning) existence. But the view of God as timeless denies this. In that view, God isn't inside time at all. It is false to say 'God exists today', or 'God performed a miracle last week', or any such statement that applies temporal categories to God. This view was formulated most famously by Boethius, a sixth-century Christian philosopher whose views were extremely influential in the Middle Ages. He wrote:

> The fact that God is eternal is the common judgment of all rational people. So let us consider what eternity is, since this clarifies for us both God's nature and his knowledge. Eternity, then, is the complete possession all at once of unlimited life... Therefore, whatever includes and possesses the whole fullness of unlimited life at once, and is such that it lacks nothing future and has lost nothing past, is rightly considered to be eternal. And it is necessary that such a being must be in full possession of itself, always present to itself, and having the full infinity of time present to it.[5]

Aquinas agreed. He suggested that we think of God rather like someone at the top of a tall tower, watching a procession pass beneath. He can see the whole of the procession at once, and is not 'in' any part of it. Similarly, God sees the whole of history at once. So he doesn't have *fore*knowledge at all. He has eternal knowledge of all events at once.

Many theologians have had problems with this notion. For example, on the assumption that causes always temporally precede their effects, how could a being outside time cause anything? Does the concept of a timeless being even make sense in itself? Surely if something didn't exist in the past, doesn't exist now and won't exist in the future, it simply doesn't exist! Many Christians have felt that the notion of God as everlasting makes more sense and is more in line with the biblical picture of God as interacting creatively with history. The 'process theologians' we saw in the first chapter take this view.

Still, even if we accept the notion of God as eternal, it doesn't help us reconcile his knowledge with free will. We can take the argument stated earlier and simply rephrase it, so instead of saying 'God knew on Friday that I would propose on Saturday', it becomes 'On Friday, it was true that God (in his timeless eternity) knows that I propose on Saturday'. Or, to put it another way, God's timeless knowledge is just as infallible as God's temporal knowledge. If God knows timelessly all our choices, then it seems our choices cannot be changed any more than his timeless knowledge can be.

We have seen one way out of the problem – Luther's answer, which is to deny that anyone has (contra-causal) free will at all.

There is an opposite route out, which is to insist upon free will but to deny that God knows what free creatures will do. This was the answer of Faustus Socinus, an intriguing character from the sixteenth century who proposed a number of innovative theological ideas and was a major influence on the emergence of unitarianism in Poland. He argued that God was inside time, rather than outside it, and that his omniscience covers only two kinds of facts – first, necessarily true ones, such as mathematical facts, and second, facts about the past. The future is intrinsically unknowable – even to God – because it depends, in part, on the free and unknowable choices of human beings. God is still omniscient, because that means only knowing all things that *can* be known, and the future is simply unknowable whether you're omniscient or not. A similar understanding of divine omniscience has been put forward more recently by Richard Swinburne, an influential Christian philosopher. He pictures God as choosing to limit his own knowledge by creating free creatures whose actions he will be unable to predict.

Many may feel that this limits God too much. Is it compatible with the claim from Psalm 139, which we saw earlier, that God knows the inmost secrets of every heart? Perhaps – for the text suggests only that God knows what the psalmist is thinking *right now* – and this doesn't entail that he knows what the psalmist will do in the future. In fact, the Old Testament presents God as sometimes predicting the future wrongly. In Jonah 3:4, for example, the prophet predicts that Nineveh will be destroyed in forty days. There is no implication that this is a conditional prophecy. But in the event, Nineveh survives. The first chapter of Micah is a prophecy that Jerusalem will be destroyed by the Assyrians, but this, too, doesn't happen. The implication seems to be that God predicts the future on the basis of how people are behaving now – but it is still possible for people to mend their ways (perhaps in response to the prediction) and for events not to turn out as God described. And that, in turn, might suggest a model of divine knowledge similar to Socinus'.

Some theologians have gone further in limiting God's knowledge. Jerome, for example, argued that it is ridiculous to suppose that God knows how many fish there are in the sea, or how many gnats are being born at this precise moment (although Matthew 10:29–30 suggests that God does know mundane things like this). Such things, thought Jerome, are unworthy of the divine attention. But in fact most Christians have believed that God knows not only these things but even more. They do not conceive of God as a sort of passive observer of history, like Aquinas' man in a tower watching a procession pass beneath. On the contrary, they think of God as actively *controlling* history. And this creates an even more pressing problem for the notion of human freedom.

Free Will and Divine Grace

Christians traditionally believe that God is sovereign over his creation: he has not simply created it and then left it to run itself (as the eighteenth-century deists believed), but he actively controls it even now. This is the Christian doctrine of providence. John Calvin wrote:

> First, then, let the reader remember that the providence we mean is not one by which the Deity, sitting idly in heaven, looks on at what is taking place in the world, but one by which, as it were, he holds the reins and overrules all events. Hence his providence extends not less to the hand than to the eye. When Abraham said to his son, 'God will provide' [Genesis 22:8], he meant not merely to assert that the future event was foreknown to God but to give up the management of an unknown business to the will of him whose job it is to bring perplexed and dubious matters to a happy result. Hence it appears that providence consists in action.[6]

Calvin believed that this divine providence basically directs everything that happens, including human actions. In particular, whether an individual person responds to God's grace has been predestined by God.

The Catholic Church, meanwhile, accepted Calvin's premise about divine providence, but it denied his conclusion about predestination. It had always sought to maintain *both* that human (and divine) acts are performed freely, *and* that all these acts occur in accordance with God's plan. Somehow, every person's choices are the choices that God wants them to make, and at the same time people do genuinely choose what they do, and are responsible for their actions. Over a thousand years before Calvin, Origen had written:

> I will say that while God preserves the free will of each man he makes use of the evil of bad men for the ordering of the whole, making them useful to the universe; yet such a man is none the less guilty, and as such he has been appointed to perform a function which is repulsive to the individual but beneficial to the whole.[7]

One point, not always appreciated, needs to be made at the outset. If we define the doctrine of providence in this way – that everything that happens does so precisely in accordance with God's will – then that precludes any use of the free will defence as a solution to the problem of evil. As we saw earlier, the idea behind the free will defence is that God gives (contra-causal) free will to his creatures, even though this is likely to result in evil and suffering. The reason is that free will is so good it outweighs all the negative consequences that will come from it. However, if we believe that all events in history – including all human actions – are the events that God wants to happen, then this move doesn't resolve anything. The claim now is that, even if there is free will, the various evil acts that human beings have committed are the ones that God wanted them to commit. In which case, the question remains open – why would God want that? And to answer *that*, we need some other explanation, like the ones we looked at in chapter 3: that God can bring greater good out of these evil acts, for example. In which case, the free will defence simply collapses into some other defence, which means that we might as well not bother with it in the first place.

This is so even if, together with the doctrine of divine sovereignty, one also maintains a belief in contra-causal free will. But doing that brings its own problems. We have already seen that simply reconciling free will and omniscience is hard enough. Once we bring in the notion that everything happens in accordance with God's own will, it seems even harder to reconcile all this! The problem is often referred to as that of grace (as opposed to omniscience) and free will: how do we reconcile the claim that human acts are free with the claim that God graciously determines what happens? The problem becomes most acute when the acts we are talking about are acts of faith towards God himself. Consider the following passage by Paul:

> We know that all things work together for good for those who love God, who are called according to his purpose. For those whom he foreknew he also predestined to be conformed to the image of his Son, in order that he might be the firstborn within a large family. And those whom he predestined he also called; and those whom he called he also justified; and those whom he justified he also glorified.
> **Romans 8:28–30**

This passage suggests that God simply predestines people to be saved (and, perhaps, others to be damned). And that implies that people do not have the ability to determine for themselves whether or not they are saved – they are simply 'called'. Paul implies that if you are called, you are justified and glorified; there is no notion here that you can be called but decide not to respond. But in Romans 3:24, Paul wrote that people are 'justified freely by [God's] grace through the redemption that is in Christ Jesus'. If justification requires God's grace, and is predestined by God, how can it be a free act on the part of the person being justified? It can be free if we define free will in a compatibilist way, as Calvin did. But Christians who defend contra-causal free will have been pulled in two directions at once when trying to explain passages such as these. On the one hand, God's grace is offered to all as a free gift, and it is up to the individual to accept it or not (without being determined by God or by anything else). But on the other, God's grace *is* somehow determining – the fact that one person accepts it (and, perhaps, the fact that another person rejects it) is part of God's plan, for God's will cannot be thwarted.

These different ideas seem simply contradictory. And, indeed, this has been arguably the most persistent problem in the entire history of Christian doctrine. It was first seriously discussed at length in the early fifth century, as part of the dispute between Augustine and Pelagius. Pelagius believed that God's grace was external to the individual: God has given us the Ten Commandments and the teaching of Jesus, and the ability to choose good or evil. This is his grace, and it is up to us to respond by doing what is right. But Augustine argued that this would mean that we save ourselves. He offered instead an understanding of God's grace as internal to the individual: God actually directs the human heart towards himself. Pelagius' condemnation by Rome, and Augustine's later canonization, meant that this would become the orthodox understanding of the matter. But the lingering influence of Pelagius in Gaul meant that, after the fall of Rome, the problem of grace and free will was vigorously debated in that region. Theologians such as Vincent of Lérins, Prosper of Aquitaine and Faustus of Riez – largely forgotten today except to specialists – wrote lengthy treatises trying to find a way through the tangle. They didn't succeed. Three centuries later, the debate was resuscitated in a huge row over a monk named Gottschalk of Orbais, who denied the existence of free will. He was condemned by his bishop, Hincmar of Reims, and virtually every theologian of the time had something to say on the matter – but once again the debate petered out without really reaching a conclusion, except that Gottschalk's doctrine of predestination (which was similar to Calvin's) was just as unacceptable as the opposite doctrine of Pelagianism.

Molinism

The debate reached its high point in the sixteenth century. In Catholic Spain, with its excellent universities, the traditions of medieval-style philosophy and theology remained dominant for longer than they did elsewhere in Europe. Here, an enormous debate broke out between two major religious orders, the Jesuits and the Dominicans. Relations between the two were generally poor during this period, and the argument about grace and free will did not help.

The debate was triggered by Luis de Molina, a retired university professor. In 1588 he published a book with the terrifying title *The Reconciliation of Free Will with the Bestowal of Grace, Divine Foreknowledge, Providence, Predestination, and Damnation, from the*

First Part of St Thomas' Articles. The book itself was just as intimidating as the title suggested, since not only were Molina's ideas extremely complex but his writing style left much to be desired. Today, the book is hardly ever read, but it does contain arguably the most subtle and clever attempt ever made to solve the problem of grace and free will.

Molina frames his account in the jargon that had been developed by earlier scholastic theologians. He distinguishes between God's *natural* knowledge and his *free* knowledge. This distinction is actually quite simple. Some things are true irrespective of God's will (for example, most Christian theologians – with one or two notable exceptions – have thought that 2 + 2 = 4 is true, quite apart from anything God does). These things are necessarily true, and God knows these things as part of his natural knowledge. But other things are true only because God wills them (for example, the fact that the world exists). He knows these things as part of his free knowledge (because they are, in a sense, knowledge of his own free acts: God knows that the world exists because he knows that he has created it).

Now, Molina accepts Aquinas' belief that God is outside time, so it makes no sense to talk about God knowing some things before he knows others. But we can talk about some items of God's knowledge *logically* preceding others. They are, as it were, more fundamental. And he suggests that God's natural knowledge logically precedes his free knowledge. It works like this. God's natural knowledge contains knowledge of possibilities. At the time Molina was writing, philosophers were developing the notion of 'possible worlds' – descriptions of different ways that the world *could* have been, although it isn't. For example, there is a possible world in which Napoleon did not invade Prussia, a possible world in which cats have six legs, and so on. It is necessarily true that each of these things is possible. And this means that God knows about these possibilities as part of his natural knowledge (which is knowledge of necessary truths). However, God also knows which of these possibilities is real. It is the possible world in which Napoleon did invade Prussia, cats have four legs, and all the other things are true which actually are true. Of course, the reason why this possible world (and not a different one) is actual is because God made it so. We are to think of God, on the eve of creation, as browsing a sort of catalogue of all the possible worlds, and picking one to actualize. Of course, it happens eternally rather than shortly before the moment of creation, but this is the basic idea. And this means that God's knowledge of what is *actually* the case is part of his free knowledge, because it is true only because God chooses that it is true.

So God has two kinds of knowledge – natural and free. God's knowledge of possibilities is part of his natural knowledge, and his knowledge of actualities is part of his free knowledge. But what about the free choices of free creatures? Molina suggests that when God surveys all the possible worlds that he could create, this includes a survey of all the possible free creatures that he could create, and the free choices that they would make were he to create them. But this is not part of his natural knowledge (because that is knowledge of necessary truths, and the choices of free creature are not necessary). It isn't part of his free knowledge either, because that is knowledge only of what is *actually* the case. Molina therefore dubs it 'middle knowledge'. It is knowledge of what free creatures *would* do *if* God were to create them.

So God is faced with a number of possible creatures that he could create (presumably there is an infinite number of them). For every one of these possible creatures, he knows what it would choose to do in any given circumstance. This is his middle knowledge, which is neither natural (because it is not knowledge of necessity) nor free (because it does not depend upon his will). God decides to create the creature Judas. Once created, Judas makes the decision to betray Christ. God always knew (as part of his middle knowledge) that Judas would make this decision if he created him; but his knowledge that Judas actually does make this decision is part of his free knowledge, since the fact that Judas actually betrays Christ depends upon the fact that God decides to create Judas in the first place. However, none of this militates against the freedom of Judas' choice to betray Christ. God doesn't *force* Judas to do it. God does want Christ to be betrayed, but he achieves this by creating a creature that he knows will freely choose to betray Christ, not by creating a creature and only then addressing the problem of how to get it to choose to betray Christ.

In particular, Molina stresses repeatedly that God's middle knowledge does not cause creatures to choose what they choose. On the contrary, God knows that Judas would choose to betray Christ because Judas would choose to do that, not vice versa. Similarly, he knows (through his free knowledge) that Judas chooses to betray Christ because Judas *does* choose that. Molina concludes:

> From this it clearly follows that no prejudice at all is done to freedom of choice or to the contingency of things by God's foreknowledge, a foreknowledge through which, because of the infinite and wholly unlimited perfection and acumen of his intellect, he sees with certainty what the free causes placed in any order of things will do, even though they could really, if they so willed, do the contrary; rather, even though that knowledge exists, freedom of choice and the contingency of things with respect to both parts [i.e., freedom to choose to perform the action in question or not] remain intact, just as if there were no foreknowledge.[8]

We can frame the argument in a different way, not used by Molina, but which I think expresses what he is trying to get at. The notion he is opposing is the idea that if a choice can be known, it is not free. Clearly, however, knowability is not intrinsically opposed to freedom. If I chose to perform a free act yesterday, I can be certain today that I did it, and so can other people – but that is no reason for supposing that it was not free. By the same token, then, if someone had certain knowledge that I will perform a certain act tomorrow, that would not in itself entail that I will not do that act freely. Why, then, do we have an intuition that it would? The reason lies in the way we normally get what knowledge we have of the future. We can predict future events only because we understand causation and we know that *this* cause will produce *that* effect. Thus, we cannot predict genuinely free acts because this way of doing so is not open to us, since they are not caused in this way. Any act which we could predict perfectly by this means could not be free.

But God's knowledge, according to Molina, doesn't work like this. As he is outside time, a free act performed tomorrow is to him no different from one performed yesterday, and his knowledge of it does nothing to harm its freedom. More fundamentally, God's middle knowledge tells him what any possible creature would do under any possible circumstances, and his free knowledge tells him which of these creatures he has chosen to actualize. In none of this does he interfere with creatures' freedom in any way or determine their choices. As a result, God knows perfectly what every creature chooses to do at every moment in time, but they still choose it freely. The reason, once again, is that an act is free if it is not causally determined; but this is compatible with being known by God.

Once people had worked out what Molina was trying to say, it became highly controversial. Molina had been raised by the Jesuits, and many Jesuit theologians supported his theory. But many Dominicans attacked it (Aquinas had been a Dominican, and they seem to have resented Molina's attempt to reinterpret Aquinas in support of his own position). In particular, the Dominican theologian Domingo Bañez argued that Molina's position was heretical. He suggested, instead, that the free acts of human beings are simply determined by God. So how are they free? Bañez's answer is that because free acts are not strictly necessary (in the sense that $2 + 2 = 4$ is necessarily true), that is enough for us to call them free, even though they are caused by God. In Molina's view, this was an inadequate answer. When an apple falls from a tree, that event is not logically necessary either, but we wouldn't say that the apple has free will. But Bañez doesn't offer any account of how human beings are any freer than falling apples.

The row between the two groups intensified, and both appealed to Rome to settle the matter once and for all. In 1597, Pope Clement VIII set up a special commission to investigate the issue of grace and free will. Ten years later, Pope Paul V dissolved the commission. He ruled that a definitive judgment would be forthcoming in good time, but meanwhile, everyone was to consider both views as acceptable alternatives. Four hundred years later, the Catholic Church is still awaiting the final ruling.

A Problem with No Answer?

The unwillingness of the Vatican to make a final pronouncement on Molina and Bañez partly reflects, perhaps, the sheer difficulty of the problem and of the proposed solutions to it. But it also reflects the belief of the Catholic Church that it doesn't really matter which of them was right, even assuming that one of them was. The solution to the problem of how to reconcile grace and free will is not something that people need to know for the sake of salvation. To put it another way, it does not really matter if we are wrong about it. From a Catholic point of view, the fact is that grace and free will are both real, and provided we believe that, we can believe what we like about the mechanics of how they can both operate at the same time.

Nevertheless, such a conclusion will not appeal to everyone, and certainly not to those who conclude that grace and free will simply are incompatible, at least as the Catholic Church defines them. As I have suggested above, this has been, historically, one of the longest-running arguments in Christian history. One way out is to follow Calvin and simply deny the existence of contra-causal free will, affirming that compatibilist free will is all that anyone either has or needs. An alternative is to do the opposite and deny that there is any irresistible grace: God freely gives free will to human beings, but in so doing he limits his own powers. In particular, God cannot force them to do what he wants, at least not without overriding their free will. Today, it seems that both of these alternatives to the Catholic line have become quite popular. Many secular philosophers – perhaps a majority – believe that compatibilist free will is the better definition of free will. This is partly because contra-causal free will is rather hard to define and imagine, and partly because it is hard to see what is so desirable about it. There is also the problem that there seems no particular reason to believe that it exists; and, indeed, it is hard to imagine what evidence there could be for either its existence or its non-existence – it is an unfalsifiable theory and therefore, perhaps, not a very meaningful one. The eighteenth-century American Reformed theologian Jonathan Edwards devoted considerable energy to arguing for this conclusion, and many Christians since (including many not in the Reformed tradition) have been convinced that he – and Calvin – were right. But, at the same time, there is today also a widespread belief among Christians in the opposite approach: to affirm free will and deny overriding grace.

Many Christians believe this for the same reason that Justin Martyr did: a basic conviction that the ability to do other than one actually does is essential to responsibility and therefore to morality. The other major reason for the prevalence of this view today is the widespread use of the free will defence in tackling the problem of evil. Despite the fashionability in some theological circles of the 'Irenaean defence', which we saw in chapter 3, the more familiar Augustinian use of free will has remained the most common response to the problem of evil at the popular level. But, as we have seen, such a defence requires the existence of contra-causal free will; it also requires abandoning the traditional doctrine of God's active providence, at least if we mean by that the notion that whatever happens is what God wants to happen. If that is so, then it seems that the debate over free will, providence, grace and the problem of evil is unlikely to end any time soon.

Chapter 7

Can There be Such a Thing as Life After Death?

'If there is no resurrection of the dead,' thundered the apostle Paul, '… then our proclamation has been in vain and your faith has been in vain.' And he's not been alone in this view. Belief in a life after death has always been central to Christianity, and indeed this is one of the central notions it shares with most other religions, in one form or another.

The idea that, after our death, we go on to somewhere else is still deeply ingrained in our culture, even as the power of traditional Christianity ebbs away. In fact, some surveys suggest that belief in life after death has actually risen in Britain over the past twenty years, with perhaps 40 per cent of people saying they believe in it. In America, meanwhile, those who expect to survive their own death are in a majority.

But is this belief rational? Does it even make sense? Isn't death something that – by definition – we *can't* survive? In this chapter we look at some of the reasons there might be for believing in life after death, and what we might mean by the idea in the first place.

Why Believe in Life after Death?

Near-death Experiences
One reason that many people give for believing in life after death is the fact that some individuals seem to have experienced it. Occasionally, critically ill people report a 'near-death experience' –

an experience of, apparently, dying. The accounts vary but often include elements such as floating above their own body, as if they were literally leaving it, seeing a bright light, being able to think more clearly than usual or even being able to transmit thoughts, and a strong positive emotion. When they recover, these people believe that what they experienced was a brief taste of life after death.

How seriously should we take these reports? They are certainly real experiences – but are they evidence of life after death? Those who say that they are point to the fact that there is a certain uniformity among them, even though the people who report them may come from different religious backgrounds. Of course, this simply means that it is likely that all or most of these experiences have some common cause. And that may well be a perfectly natural cause – for example, it has been argued that, under certain circumstances when death is near, the brain may produce various chemicals that induce euphoria and hallucination.

Similarly, it should be remembered that, although there are certain similarities between near-death experiences, they seem to vary according to religious tradition. For example, Christians are far more likely to report a meeting with God than people with no religion. So it seems that one's own religious background does, to a certain extent, determine the form of one's near-death experience, and this suggests that its causes lie at least partly within oneself.

On the other hand, those who believe that these experiences really are supernatural point to the evidence that those who undergo them return with knowledge that they could not otherwise have had. There are plenty of stories of people 'leaving' their bodies and going on a quick trip around the hospital before being resuscitated, and subsequently describing things in other rooms that really existed but which they could not have seen. If this phenomenon could be repeated under test conditions it would be powerful evidence for something paranormal going on – but of course it would be very hard, not to say inadvisable, to try to create a near-death experience!

Apart from all this, there is one main problem with using near-death experiences as evidence for life after death, and that is the fact that those undergoing them do not actually die. They are, after all, *near*-death experiences. At the very most, they tell us what people experience at the point of death; they cannot, by definition, tell us what happens *after* death.

It might be added that most people who report near-death experiences seem to describe a heavenly experience of euphoria. Not many people seem willing to own up to going to hell – and of those who do, most are Christians!

Mediums

One powerful reason which inclines many people to believe in life after death is the existence of mediums, that is, people who claim to be able to contact the dead. In most of the philosophical literature on this subject, the evidence of mediums is generally either ignored or dismissed out of hand as obviously fraudulent, but this attitude fails to take into account how powerful this evidence can be, at least when it is experienced first-hand. Often, when describing what they claim they are being told by the dead, mediums do seem to possess knowledge that they could not have otherwise known. If this is so, then it seems to be good evidence for the claim that people not only continue to exist after death but retain their characters and memories and are able to communicate with (at least some) living persons. It is also evidence that the dead continue to care about those whom they cared about in life, since the messages that mediums pass on are typically from close relatives of their clients and express concern for them.

When modern mediumship became fashionable in the nineteenth century, many mediums were indeed frauds, and their charlatanry was often quite crude. There are certainly deliberately fraudulent mediums today, too. But I do not think that any serious examination of modern mediums will support the claim that they *all* are. On the contrary, most mediums are convinced that they are genuinely contacting the dead. Could they be sincere but mistaken? This wouldn't explain the fact that mediums seem to have knowledge that they couldn't have had without contacting the dead. For example, they may state that their client's grandfather died of a certain illness, or know his name – things they couldn't know unless, as they claim, the grandfather himself is invisibly present and giving them this information. One major problem here is that such evidence is invariably anecdotal: mediums rarely submit to scientific testing, and when they do, the results are always inconclusive. This does not mean that the evidence is worthless; simply branding evidence 'anecdotal' may weaken it compared with evidence acquired in a laboratory, but it does not mean it is false, simply that one should be that much more sceptical about it. Moreover, mediums themselves often explain the lack of results in scientific tests as an intrinsic feature of their work. The spirits, it seems, only speak in order to improve people's lives or to pass on important information to relatives; they are not interested in proving to scientists that they exist. This seems almost too convenient to be true, but that doesn't mean that it *isn't* true.

If we take even the anecdotal evidence seriously, though, it does not at all prove that mediums have actually spoken with the dead. For one thing, mediums (especially the more familiar ones from television) often work with a large audience; whatever 'knowledge' they think they are getting from the spirits, there is bound to be someone in that audience who recognizes it – especially if it is vague enough. When working with a single client, they may also use 'cold reading', where the reader responds to the client's body language or other subconscious signals and tailors the reading accordingly. This may explain some of it, but perhaps not all – for mediums also sometimes come up with extremely detailed knowledge that surely cannot be the result of lucky guesses or reactions to the client's body language. David Hume argued that, when faced with an apparent miracle, it is always more reasonable to suppose that there is a natural explanation, however improbable, because nothing could be more improbable than a miracle. Perhaps that reasoning could apply here: even if we grant that mediums do seem to have knowledge that they could not have except by contacting the dead, we could imagine other means of gaining that knowledge which, although unlikely, are *less* unlikely. Perhaps mediums have some kind of psychic ability which allows them to gain knowledge directly from the minds of their clients, and they misinterpret this as speaking to the dead. That is certainly very improbable, but still it is perhaps less improbable than the notion that there are dead souls floating around us all the time, audible (or visible) only to a select few.

Christians have differed over whether mediumship is possible and how to interpret it. In the Old Testament, 1 Samuel 28:8–25 contains a famous scene of mediumship, where King Saul contacts a witch of Endor and has her summon the spirit of the prophet Samuel. In the story, Samuel seems unhappy at being summoned and gives Saul a fairly gloomy prophecy. In late antiquity, Christians argued over whether the witch of Endor was a genuine medium: had she really summoned the dead prophet, as the text suggests, or was the spirit actually a demon pretending to be Samuel? Whatever the truth, Christians agreed that it had been a bad idea.

Many modern Christians share the traditional mistrust of mediums, based on biblical condemnations of the practice and a belief that any spiritual forces contacted in this way will be demonic. But added to this is the fact that the picture offered by mediums has little in common with what Christians believe. As we shall see, the traditional Christian belief is that the soul, after death, goes somewhere else – heaven or hell, perhaps – to await the final resurrection. But most mediums present us with a picture of dead spirits as still intimately concerned with earthly matters, either watching, communicating and interfering from some ethereal plane of existence, or hanging around invisibly on earth. Moreover, these spirits say little of God and instead send messages almost entirely about the living – encouragements, warnings and so on.

In effect, then, it is possible that mediumship provides evidence for life after death. However, the evidence is of variable quality, it is hard to confirm, it could be explained by other means, and even if compelling it does not corroborate the Christian view of life after death.

Morality

One important argument for believing in life after death was set out most famously by the philosopher Immanuel Kant at the end of the eighteenth century. In his *Critique of Practical Reason*, Kant argues that good actions can only count as good if they are performed with the *intention* of doing good. In fact, they must be done with the intention of bringing about the *ultimate* good. Otherwise, we'd just be doing them because we happen to be nice people, and not because we are concerned with what is truly good. But that can only make sense if the ultimate good will actually come about. Since it is fairly clear that the ultimate good is not coming about in this life, it follows that it will happen in the next life. Otherwise, morality would be simply impossible.

It has to be said that there are some problems with this argument: for one thing, we might say that it is perfectly possible to do good actions, *hoping* to bring about the ultimate good, even if that ultimate good never actually comes about. The argument essentially assumes that the universe is an intrinsically moral place, and that good will triumph. A cruder version of the argument assumes this even more explicitly. The wicked are not punished and the virtuous are not rewarded in this life, so there must be another life where they meet their just deserts. But why should the universe work in this way? The fact that we would like it to do so is hardly any guarantee that it does.

God

We could turn the argument around in this way: suppose that we already believe that God exists, and that he is good. Is it not reasonable that he will ensure that there is life after death? This argument can take several different forms. It may be that God's justice demands that the wicked are punished and the virtuous rewarded after death. However, it's important to remember that, from a Christian point of view, a person's destination after death is determined not by what kind of life they have lived, but by God's grace. So the appeal to God's justice would not work within this context.

Alternatively, it may be that God's love for his people means that he will never abandon them to non-existence. Perhaps, for example, if he truly values his relationship with them, he will not allow them to perish. Some thinkers dispute this, however. They point out that if something is significant, it is significant irrespective of how long it lasts: why would our lives be any more meaningful if they were indefinitely prolonged? Indeed, sometimes things are considered *more* meaningful or beautiful if they last only a short time. In Japanese culture, it is the very fact that cherry blossom is so fleeting that makes it beautiful.

All the same, whilst it might not be very meaningful from a cosmic point of view whether or not we will perish utterly at our death, it certainly makes a lot of difference from *our* point of view. And if God really cares about us, it might seem reasonable that he would not abandon us to oblivion. So if we believe in a loving God, it is quite reasonable to believe in life after death too.

But what *is* life after death? And could it really be possible?

Two Different Approaches

The traditional Christian understanding of life after death is rather strange, in that it is a mixture of two quite different approaches to the issue. One of these comes from ancient Greek philosophy, and the other is inherited from Judaism.

The Immortal Soul

Perhaps the most common way of thinking of life after death is to say that human beings have an immortal soul, an immaterial 'self' that survives the death of the body. The belief has rarely been expressed more clearly than by one of its earliest exponents, the ancient Greek philosopher Plato.

In his dialogue *Phaedo*, Plato presents us with a dramatic situation. His hero, Socrates, has been condemned to death for his unconventional beliefs. His friends come to visit him in prison, to find to their horror that he is to be executed later that day. But, surprisingly, Socrates himself does not seem bothered by the news. He explains that the reason he is not afraid is that he knows that, although his body may die, his soul will survive. He talks to his friend Cebes:

Socrates: Since what cannot die cannot be destroyed, isn't it the case that the soul, if it is immortal, must also be imperishable?
Cebes: Most certainly.
Socrates: Then when death attacks a man, the part of him that dies does just that, but the immortal part escapes death and is preserved safe and sound?
Cebes: True.
Socrates: Then, Cebes, beyond question, the soul is immortal and imperishable, and our souls will really exist in another world![1]

Socrates has to tell his friends off shortly afterwards, when they ask
how he wants to be buried. He reminds them that *he* won't be buried
at all. He – that is, his soul – will be somewhere else, and it makes no
difference to him what they do with the body he leaves behind.

The Resurrection of the Dead

While Plato and other Greek philosophers were developing the idea
of the immortality of the soul, a quite different tradition was
appearing among Jewish writers and theologians. Early Judaism
lacked any real idea of either the soul or life after death. The nearest
it came was something called *Sheol*, which has been translated
variously as 'hell', 'the grave', or 'the pit'. Psalm 88:4–5 draws a
picture of what may be expected there:

> I am counted among those who go down to the Pit;
> I am like those who have no help,
> Like those forsaken among the dead,
> Like the slain that lie in the grave,
> Like those whom you remember no more,
> For they are cut off from your hand.

In Psalm 94:17 Sheol is 'the land of silence', and in Job 10:21–22 we
hear of 'the land of gloom and deep darkness, the land of gloom and
chaos, where light is like darkness'. Sheol certainly doesn't sound
much fun; it is something to be avoided, little different from
complete annihilation. In this view, the early Hebrews were similar
to other Middle Eastern cultures; the epic of Gilgamesh, for
example, describes dead souls as sitting mournfully in the land of
the dead like great, drab birds.

As Judaism developed, however, the prospect lightened
considerably. Some Jewish traditions considered the possibility that,
although there may be no life after death to speak of in the normal
run of things, God might miraculously bring someone back to life
on earth. In fact, they came to believe that God would do precisely
this for everyone at the end of time. In Daniel, which scholars
believe to be one of the last books of the Old Testament to be
written, we find the following passage at the culmination of a
graphic description of the end of the world:

> Many of those who sleep in the dust of the earth shall awake,
> some to everlasting life, and some to shame and everlasting
> contempt. Those who are wise shall shine like the brightness of
> the sky, and those who lead many to righteousness, like the stars
> for ever and ever.
> **Daniel 12:2–3**

Indeed, in the last verse of the book, Daniel himself is told, 'you, go your way, and rest; you shall rise for your reward at the end of the days'. On this conception, then, when we're dead, we're dead and there is no happy afterlife for our souls (even assuming that we have souls in the first place). But God will miraculously raise us from the dead in the future.

The Christian Combination

When Jesus lived, the notion of the resurrection of the dead was not uncontroversial in Judaism. Some, such as the Pharisees, believed that it would be one of the most important events of the end of the world. Others, such as the Sadducees, did not believe it would happen. Indeed, in Matthew 22:23–33, Jesus is quizzed on the subject by some Sadducees, who clearly lump him together with the Pharisees. Jesus' answer is ambiguous, but he does seem to agree with the Pharisees that the dead will rise.

Before long, however, belief in the resurrection of the dead at the end of time would become Jewish orthodoxy, and it would remain so. It is one of *The Thirteen Principles of Faith*, a kind of summary of the fundamental doctrines of Judaism written by the twelfth-century Jewish philosopher, Maimonides.

Christianity also inherited the doctrine. In particular, Christians recognized that it might help them to understand what had happened to Jesus. As with so much else, the doctrine was pioneered by Paul, who as a Pharisee believed that the resurrection of the dead was one of the signs of the end of the world. In chapter 15 of 1 Corinthians, he links the resurrection of Christ very closely to the general resurrection of the whole of humanity. He calls Christ's resurrection 'the first fruits': Christ is, as it were, the trailblazer, opening the path that everyone else will follow shortly.

This notion of the resurrection of the body, inherited from Judaism, quickly became one of the most distinctive features of Christianity compared with other religions and philosophies in the Roman empire. Philosophers laughed at its crudity compared with the Platonic doctrine of the immortality of the soul; to them, Christians were simple people who were unable to turn their minds away from the physical world and contemplate God without having to have a crucified criminal help them out.

But many Christians were themselves Platonists. The Platonic belief in a higher, spiritual realm, to which the soul might ascend through moral living and spiritual contemplation, appealed to them, and they felt that Christianity shared this approach to life. So they too believed in the immortality of the soul. Notably, some Christian writers rejected the notion that the soul is *naturally* immortal, arguing instead that it survives the death of the body only because God gives it the special ability to do so; left to its own devices, it would perish just as the body does. Justin Martyr and Tatian were among those with this view. Nevertheless, by the time of Augustine in the fourth and fifth centuries, a fairly standard Platonic understanding of the soul's immortality had become virtually universal, adopted alongside the traditional belief in the resurrection of the body. This meant that a rather complex doctrine quickly appeared: at death, the body and soul separate, the body to disintegrate and the soul to live on, in good Platonic fashion. But the soul then enters a sort of dormant period, until at the end of time the body is raised up again, and the body and soul are reunited. Some theologians thought that the soul, while it was waiting for the resurrection, might experience a sort of foretaste of what awaited it afterwards. So Augustine tells us:

> As for what happens after death, there's nothing wrong with saying that death is good to the good, and evil to the evil. For the spirits of righteous people which have been separated from their bodies are at rest; but those of the wicked are punished until their bodies rise again. The bodies of the just will rise to life everlasting, and of the others to death eternal, which is called the second death.[2]

So immediately after death, the soul goes somewhere fairly pleasant, if it is a good soul, or somewhere extremely undesirable, if it is a bad

one. But this is a sort of stop-gap, because the souls have not yet
been properly judged. That happens only at the end of time, once all
the souls have been reunited with their bodies; and then they are
sent to their final destinations. It is a picture that could receive
support from the parable of Lazarus and the rich man, told by Jesus
in Luke 16:19–31. The two characters here are described as going to
their reward and punishment immediately after death. And indeed,
in Philippians 1:23, Paul speaks of his desire to depart the flesh and
be with Christ, apparently in the belief that he would go to Christ
immediately after his death.

It seems, then, that the traditional Christian picture is a rather
bizarre mingling of two quite different understandings of life after
death. Need it be this way? Certainly not – most Christian
thinkers have preferred to emphasize one approach rather than the
other, and some have completely eradicated one of them. In late
antiquity, for example, some Christians – influenced by Origen,
but taking his ideas further – were accused of denying the
resurrection of the body altogether and talking only of the soul.
At the other extreme, in the sixteenth century, Martin Luther
argued that the notion of the immortal soul was an unbiblical and
essentially pagan doctrine, and he therefore believed only in the
resurrection of the body, as the Pharisees had. In fact, he
denounced the doctrine of the immortality of the soul as a
'monstrosity' of the Catholic faith. After all, in the passage from
1 Corinthians quoted at the start of this chapter, Paul said that the
Christian faith revolved around *resurrection* – and he would hardly
have said that if the soul were immortal anyway! Matthew Tyndale,
one of the first translators of the Bible into English and a follower
of Luther, expressed his view like this:

> The true faith putteth the resurrection, which we be warned to look
> for every hour. The heathen philosophers, denying that, did put that
> the souls did ever live. And the pope joineth the spiritual doctrine of
> Christ and the fleshly doctrine of philosophers together; things so
> contrary that they cannot agree, no more than the Spirit and the
> flesh do in a Christian man. And because the fleshly-minded pope
> consenteth unto heathen doctrine, therefore he corrupteth the
> Scripture to establish it.[3]

Many modern theologians have agreed. Karl Barth commented:

> What is the meaning of the Christian hope in this life? A life after
> death? An event apart from death? A tiny soul which, like a
> butterfly, flutters away above the grave and is still preserved
> somewhere, in order to live on immortally? That was how the
> heathen looked on the life after death. But that is not the Christian
> hope. 'I believe in the resurrection of the body.' Body in the Bible
> is quite simply man, man, moreover, under the sign of sin, man laid
> low. And to this man it is said, Thou shalt rise again.[4]

So why have Christians chosen to go one way or the other? We can
see if we compare the two approaches in a little more detail.

The Soul or the Body?

The Immortal Soul

At first glance, the doctrine of the immortality of the soul seems to
make quite a lot of sense. It is easy to understand, and it is
comforting to think that someone who has just died has gone
immediately to a better place, and is probably having a much nicer
time than those who are left behind. It is certainly this idea that
people most commonly mean by 'life after death'.

But this doctrine does rely on there being a soul that could
survive the body. And that notion is very hard to defend. There are
well-known philosophical objections to the theory, which have
been sufficient to convince most philosophers that there is no soul
that can exist without a body: how could such a soul interact with
the body in the first place? Moreover, if there is a soul that thinks,
it is hard to see what the brain is for. Cognitive scientists are
increasingly able to map cognitive functions to different parts of
the brain. If certain parts of the brain do not work, we become
unable to do certain kinds of mental acts. This suggests strongly
that our mental lives are explicable solely in terms of brain
functions. It does not prove it, certainly. Perhaps there is a soul
which, for some reason, needs the brain in order to think, just as a

musician needs an instrument to play. But what reason might we have for supposing such a thing? Isn't the simpler explanation usually the right one?

We can flesh this out if we think about what a soul that would survive the body would actually be like. Those who believe in the soul generally describe it as spiritual and immaterial, but it is not always easy to say what this really means, except that it is different from physical things. So what would life be like for such a soul after it had left the body? Clearly it would not be able to do anything that requires a body, such as moving, seeing or hearing anything, or acting on the world in any way. Indeed, if cognitive science is to be believed, then imagination, memory and thought itself all require a brain. What is there left for a soul to do? Its existence would be an utterly lonely and inert one. And even if we accept this picture, then it is hard to see how the soul would, in any meaningful way, be the same person as the one who died. We identify ourselves by our memories, our character and our friends. If the soul that survives death has none of these, in what way is it us? It would be like having your appendix removed and saying that *that* is you.

All of these considerations lead many modern philosophers and theologians to reject the notion of the immortal soul as unattractive, quite apart from its implausibility. But it might be possible to turn these points on their head. What if we were to say that abandoning the things of this world – the body and its distractions, emotions and imagination – is what allows a soul to focus more strongly on God?

This way of thinking was very common among Christian writers in late antiquity and the Middle Ages. Indeed, they were taking their cue from Plato, who had described the soul as 'maimed' by its association with the body. Consider the following remarks by Origen, who was greatly influenced by Plato:

> If you love the flesh, you can't understand spiritual love. But if you reject all fleshly things – I mean not just flesh and blood, but also money and wealth, the earth itself, the heavens themselves, for all that will pass away – if you have rejected all that, and if your soul is no longer bound by any of it, and if you are not trapped by any love of vice, then you can understand spiritual love.[5]

For Origen, a true Christian life involves gradually learning to separate oneself from the physical world and its distractions. The love of God is a radical love that calls the Christian away from attachment to anything except God himself. The same idea is expressed in uncompromising terms over a thousand years later, by an anonymous fourteenth-century English author:

> Put a cloud of forgetting beneath yourself; between you and everything that was ever created... I make no exception, whether they are physical or spiritual things, or the nature or activity of any created thing, whether good or evil. In a word, everything should be hidden under the cloud of forgetting. For although it is sometimes very useful to think about the nature and deeds of some created things, at this time it is worth little or nothing. Why? Whenever you think about anything that God has made, or what those things have done... the eye of the soul is open to it and focuses on it, like the eye of an archer is fixed on his target. And I tell you this: if there is anything that you are thinking about, it is above you for as long as you think about it, and between you and your God. And you are further from God whenever anything is in your mind except God.[6]

If we are thinking in these terms, then not having a body would be a real asset. For these writers, the Christian life revolves around one thing of overriding importance: the relationship between the individual and God. They prize the notion of the immortality of the soul because it offers a way of making that relationship final. In this life, we must strive to focus on God; but after death, the disembodied soul could find nothing easier, because there will be no distractions at all. Paradoxically, despite the great difference between embodied human life and the existence of the disembodied soul, this view emphasizes the continuity between them. The soul that strives for God in this life will continue to do so after death, and will find it an easier matter. This notion of the next life actually beginning in this life has its roots, once again, in Paul:

> So we do not lose heart. Even though our outer nature is wasting away, our inner nature is being renewed day by day. For this slight momentary affliction is preparing us for an eternal weight of glory

> beyond all measure, because we look not at what can be seen but
> at what cannot be seen; for what can be seen is temporary, but
> what cannot be seen is eternal.
> **2 Corinthians 4:16–18**

According to the Eastern Orthodox tradition, this leads to a
completely new state of being for the soul. If modern philosophers
criticize the doctrine of the immortal soul for dehumanizing the
person after death, making them something quite different, then
theologians like the seventh-century Maximus the Confessor
celebrate it for exactly the same reason. For Maximus, the soul that
becomes entirely focused on God will be united with God, to such
an extent that it can actually be called God:

> When air is lit up by the sun, it seems to be light and nothing else –
> not because it stops being what it is, but because the light is so
> strong in it that we believe the whole thing to be light. In the same
> way, when human nature is united to God it can be said to be God,
> right through – not because it stops being what it is, but because it
> gets to share in divinity so much that God alone can be seen in it.[7]

The Resurrection of the Body

In light of these considerations, it might be thought that the
doctrine of the resurrection of the body does not have a lot going
for it. It seems crude and little better than science fiction; can we
really believe that a day will come when the corpses of the dead will
suddenly come back to life? Would we want to believe such a thing?

Ever since Christianity began, its defenders have been eager to
point out that such a thing is perfectly possible. In fact, in the
second century AD, when theologians such as Aristides the
Philosopher and Justin Martyr first began defending Christianity
against the criticisms of others, the plausibility of this doctrine was
one of their main topics. They argued that if God created the body
in the first place, he is quite capable of raising it up. Christians who
have taken this line have disagreed, however, over the precise nature
of *what* is raised up. Some have interpreted it in a relatively crude
way, imagining that it would be literally the same body that would
rise. This is why the practice of cremation was vehemently opposed

by many Christians for a long time, because if the body were incinerated then it could hardly be resurrected. Some, meanwhile, have wondered exactly what state the body would be in when resurrected; Thomas Aquinas believed that, no matter what their age was at the time of death, everyone would be raised in the prime of life (about thirty, he thought). What's more, any physical deficits or problems in life would be rectified in the resurrection. A person born blind would be resurrected with perfect eyesight, and (in a comment apparently designed to comfort balding men) everyone would have a splendid head of hair.

Other theologians, however, believed that there were serious difficulties with the notion of bodily resurrection in the first place. One puzzle that medieval philosophers liked to consider concerned cannibalism: suppose a cannibal tucks into a rare steak of missionary, digesting it and making it part of his own body. When they are resurrected, which of them gets that bit? In fact, isn't it true that, after death, the body disintegrates and its parts are taken into the soil and redistributed, so that they will probably return in someone else's body anyway? And don't the parts of the body get gradually replaced throughout life, just through the normal processes of living?

Paul anticipates questions like these:

But someone will ask, 'How are the dead raised? With what kind of body do they come?' Fool! What you sow does not come to life until it dies. And as for what you sow, you do not sow the body that is to be, but a bare seed, perhaps of wheat or of some other grain... So it is with the resurrection of the dead. What is sown is perishable, what is raised is imperishable. It is sown in dishonour, it is raised in glory. It is sown in weakness, it is raised in power. It is sown a physical body, it is raised a spiritual body.

1 Corinthians 15:35–44

Paul's argument seems to suggest that the body that dies is exactly the same one that rises again, but he stresses that it has been fundamentally changed; it is no longer a physical body, but a spiritual one. Where Plato thought of a mortal body and an immortal soul co-existing, with one dying and the other surviving eternally, Paul thinks instead of a mortal body that is *transformed* into an immortal one. In other words, thinking in terms of 'holy zombies' is ridiculous. The resurrection body will be quite different in nature from the body that we have now – it will not even be physical.

If this is so, we might reasonably ask in what way it is the *same* body. It won't be made out of the same stuff as the body we have now. That in itself is no hindrance to its being the same body: as we saw, the parts of the body are replaced throughout life anyway, and it is still the same body. But that is a gradual process; if every part of the body were to be replaced at once, there would be problems. And that's even more so if we consider that there is a long period of time between the death of the old body and the raising of the new one. It is sometimes asked how comforting it would really be to think that, although I die, one day in the future a new me will come into being – exactly like me in every way, perhaps, and with all my memories. Wouldn't that just be a replica? Wouldn't *I*, the person I am now, still be dead?

One way around this might be to take the traditional route of combining the notion of resurrection with that of the immortality of the soul. So the future me will be the same as the present me, because the soul that I have now will return and be united to that body. It has to be said that this doesn't seem very helpful either. We have seen that a disembodied soul, if it could exist at all, would have no memory or character traits from its previous life. So having it return to a body wouldn't make that body *me*, any more than donating a kidney to someone else makes that person me.

A better approach would be simply to appeal to divine omnipotence. If God is omnipotent, he can do anything that is possible. And it is certainly possible to imagine oneself dying, and then being raised in a new form at some time in the future. It might even be possible to imagine that this new form is a non-physical one, although what that really means is not easy to say.

What advantages are there to this way of thinking of life after death? One major advantage is that it doesn't commit us to any particular understanding of human nature. It is quite compatible with denying the existence of the soul, and indeed with thorough-going materialism (just as it is also compatible with belief in the soul or dualism). From a theological point of view, however, there are two main advantages, each of which has been fundamental to the renewed interest that the doctrine of the resurrection of the body has enjoyed in recent years.

First, it affirms the importance of the body. Thinking in terms of resurrection safeguards the biblical conception of the human being as an organic whole, body as well as soul. It avoids the heretical notion of the body as evil, or as unsaveable. There has always been a tendency for the way of thinking that we saw earlier with Origen and Maximus, the elevation of the soul at the expense of the body, to slip into this. Maximus insisted that the body would be elevated together with the soul, but Origen did not.

The central Christian doctrine of the incarnation, by contrast, affirms the centrality of the body – it literally means the 'enfleshment' of God. And if Christ's resurrection is meant to be the role model for our own, then there must be a bodily element involved. According to the New Testament, the risen Christ may have been able to pass through locked doors or alter his appearance, but he could also eat and be touched.

The second advantage of thinking in terms of resurrection is related to the first. One of the features of bodily existence is living in a community with others. And, as we saw earlier, the notion of the immortality of the soul has great difficulty with this. It has certainly not been a concern of the authors quoted, whose interest is solely in the relationship between the individual and God. What of the relationship of the individual to other individuals, or of God's relationship to the community?

It is concerns like these that lead Jürgen Moltmann, one of the most prominent theologians today, to reject the notion of the immortality of the soul as selfish and intrinsically Gnostic. The Gnostics, who were very prominent in the second century, believed that salvation was a matter of escaping from the physical world, which was intrinsically evil. For Moltmann, by contrast, salvation is an inherently communal matter, one that involves the whole of creation. Indeed, it goes beyond the merely human sphere. Consider the famous words of Revelation 21:1, almost at the end of the Bible:

Then I saw a new heaven and a new earth; for the first heaven and
the first earth had passed away, and the sea was no more.

Are we to think of the new heaven and the new earth simply as a
place that God creates to put his resurrected people in, or does it
represent a fundamental belief in the value of the whole of creation,
and the role and place of all things in the future life? That may also
be Paul's thinking when he says:

When all people are subjected to him, then the Son himself will also
be subjected to the one who put all things in subjection under him,
so that God may be all in all.
1 Corinthians 15:28

In this conception, the very notion of 'life after death' becomes a
flawed way of thinking of things. Christians shouldn't be asking,
'What will happen to me when I die?' Instead they should be asking,
'How will God transform the world at the end of time – and what
will my role be?'

Chapter 8

What Happens to People from Different Religions?

In 1253, a Belgian friar named William of Rubruck arrived at the court of Möngke Khan, the absolute ruler of the Mongolian empire – the largest land-based empire of all time. William and his companions had endured untold hardships on their months-long trek from Europe into the heartlands of central Asia; exposed to the elements, and unfamiliar with the local languages, they had almost starved to death when their food ran out. William persevered, though, inspired by his audacious goal: to try to convert the Great Khan himself to Christianity.

The court of Möngke Khan was not what William expected. There were no monsters with their heads in their chests or giant feet, like the ones that European encyclopaedias confidently proclaimed inhabited Asia. Qaraqorum, the Mongolian capital, was much smaller than William expected, considering that it was the seat of the most powerful ruler in the world. And it was full of religious buildings of every kind. There were Buddhist temples, Taoist temples, mosques and even churches. Most of the rulers of the Mongolian empire still practised their traditional, shamanistic religion, but they believed in religious freedom for the peoples they conquered. Just ten years before William arrived at Qaraqorum, Batu Khan, ruler of the western Mongol 'Golden Horde', had completed the conquest of Russia and informed the princes of the Russian cities that they could continue to practise their own Christian religion provided they paid their taxes.

Möngke Khan believed in rational discussion between religions, and he was in the habit of organizing debates at his court, in which the representatives of the various religions would try to present their own faith as the most rational and criticize the others. William took part enthusiastically – but he was a complete failure. As the sole representative of Catholic Christianity, he began his preaching by insisting that everyone else (even the other Christians at court, who were members of the Persia-based Church of the East and, in Catholic eyes, heretics) were all going to hell unless they converted. The Mongols were not impressed. Möngke Khan himself told William:

> The nurse at first lets some drops of milk into the infant's mouth, so that by tasting its sweetness he may be enticed to suck; only then does she offer him her breast. In the same way you should persuade Us, whom you claim to be so totally unacquainted with this doctrine, in a simple and rational manner. Instead you immediately threaten Us with eternal punishments.[1]

On another occasion, the Great Khan explained the religious philosophy of his people:

> We Mongols believe there is but one God, by Whom we live and by Whom we die, and towards Him we have an upright heart... But just as God gave different fingers to the hand so has He given different ways to men.[2]

William's mission was an almost complete failure. The Mongols were used to the respectful exchange of religious ideas. Möngke Khan's own mother had been a Christian, who had spent much time founding Muslim universities. The exclusivist outlook of a medieval European friar was alien to them, and in 1255, considerably chastened by his experiences in the Orient, William of Rubruck returned home.

The visit of William of Rubruck to Qaraqorum illustrates a basic problem that has faced Christians throughout history. What sort of attitude should one take to other religions? Do they offer alternative routes to God? Or are they completely false? Is there any kind of compromise possible between these two extremes? This isn't just a theoretical problem. In today's multicultural world, the religious makeup of Qaraqorum is now often the norm rather than the exception. Adherents of different religions live side by side and have to get on with each other. How should they approach each other's religions?

Christian theologians today often distinguish between three basic approaches to this problem, although I shall suggest that in fact there are four. Most Christians throughout history have adopted one of these views.

Exclusivism

In his magisterial *City of God*, one of the most important Christian books ever written, Augustine of Hippo mused upon the ultimate end of humanity:

> In that final peace which all our morality refers to, and for the sake of which it is kept up, our nature will enjoy a lasting immortality and incorruption and have no more vices, and we will experience no resistance from ourselves or from others. So it will not be necessary that reason should rule vices which no longer exist, but God will rule each person, and the soul will rule the body, with a sweetness and ease suitable to the ease of a life that is done with bondage. And this state will be eternal there, and we will be certain of its eternity, and so the peace of this blessedness and the blessedness of this peace will be the supreme good... But, on the other hand, those who do not belong to this city of God will inherit eternal misery, which is also called the second death, because the soul will be separated from God, which is its life, and so it cannot be said to live, and the body will be subjected to eternal pains. And so this second death will be all the worse, because no death will end it.[3]

By 'the city of God', Augustine meant, in effect, the community of those who will be saved. He believed that this city was not exactly identical with the church – for even within the church there are evil-doers – but its borders do not extend outside the church. He agreed with the judgment of Cyprian of Carthage, a much-respected bishop and martyr of the third century. Writing about those within the church who are guilty of moral failings, Cyprian wrote:

> And do not let them think that the way of life or of salvation is still open to them, if they have refused to obey the bishops and priests, since in Deuteronomy the Lord God says, 'And the man that will do presumptuously, and will not hearken unto the priest or judge, whosoever be shall be in those days, that man shall die, and all the people shall hear and fear, and do no more presumptuously.' God commanded that those who did not obey his priests must be killed, and those who did not listen to his judges who were appointed for the time. And so they were indeed killed with the sword, when the circumcision of the flesh was still in force. But now that circumcision has begun to be of the spirit among God's faithful servants, those who are proud and arrogant are killed with the sword of the Spirit, in that they are thrown out of the church. For they cannot live out of it, since the house of God is one, and there can be no salvation to anyone except in the church.[4]

Uncompromising words! Cyprian and Augustine (especially the latter) are often cited as the architects of what is known as exclusivism: the doctrine that salvation is available only to Christians. Within that formula, however, there is quite a lot of ambiguity.

For one thing, it is not always clear who is being 'excluded'. The passage from Cyprian is talking about people who call themselves Christians but behave immorally and refuse to obey the church authorities. Augustine, too, after the passage quoted above, spends considerable time considering whether heretics and schismatics can be saved (his conclusion is that they cannot). For these writers, moreover, salvation is found only within the church – that is, the Catholic Church. For Augustine, and indeed most early Christians, the notion of a genuine Christian who was not a member of the Catholic Church was almost unthinkable. They invariably condemned 'schismatics' with as much vehemence as 'heretics', and often in the same breath – for, from their viewpoint, to be schismatic was to be heretical. Thus we find Ignatius of Antioch, one of the earliest Christian writers after the New Testament, commenting:

> Do not be deceived, my brothers. If anyone follows a maker of schism, he does not inherit the kingdom of God; if anyone walks in strange doctrine, he has no part in the passion [of Christ].[5]

The early Christians who took this line had less to say about the followers of other religions entirely. In fact, 'other religions' for the Church Fathers generally meant the pagan religion of Rome itself, and Judaism. But those who took an exclusivist line towards heretics and schismatics were generally more than happy to extend it to pagans and Jews too. The *City of God* itself is, as a whole, an attempt to demonstrate the inefficacy of paganism compared to Christianity. Augustine shared the belief of many earlier Christian writers that classical paganism was inspired by demons. The second-century theologian Tatian the Syrian, for example, had mocked the myths of the pagan Greeks and Romans, arguing that the behaviour of their 'gods' deserved disgust rather than worship. He concluded that the adherents of this religion had simply been misled by demons.

The early Christians usually had less to say about Judaism. In fact, the continued existence of Judaism as an independent religion was something of a theological puzzle for Christians, since they believed that their own religion was the fulfilment of Judaism. They believed that the promises made by God to Abraham and the other Jewish patriarchs had been fulfilled in Christ and in the church. That meant that there was plenty of truth in Judaism, if by that one meant Old Testament-era Judaism. Contemporary Judaism, on the other hand, was a different matter. Most Christian writers simply ignored the subject. One exception was Justin Martyr, who in the second century wrote a long *Dialogue with Trypho* in which he represents himself as having a friendly discussion with a Jewish philosopher (by the end of it, Trypho agrees with him that Christianity is true and in accordance with the Old Testament). John Chrysostom, who was bishop of Constantinople at the end of the fourth century, preached a series of sermons warning Christians to avoid contact with Jews. These are often cited as an early example of Christian anti-Semitism, although Chrysostom was speaking of Judaism as a religion, not of Jews as a race. After all, he venerated the ancient Jewish prophets just as much as he denounced contemporary Jewish believers. The same is true of Martin Luther, who in 1543 wrote a pamphlet entitled *On the Jews and Their Lies*. This tirade – extreme even by Luther's standards – went so far as to call for Jews to be murdered and their synagogues to be set on fire. Yet, again, Luther was attacking Jews for their beliefs rather than for anything racial. And in other (mostly earlier) writings he took a quite different attitude towards Jews. In 1523 he wrote a piece entitled *That Jesus Christ Was Born a Jew*, in which he stated:

If I had been a Jew and had seen such dolts and blockheads govern and teach the Christian faith, I would sooner have become a hog than a Christian. They have dealt with the Jews as if they were dogs rather than human beings; they have done little else than deride them and seize their property... If the apostles, who also were Jews, had dealt with us Gentiles as we Gentiles deal with the Jews, there would never have been a Christian among the Gentiles... When we are inclined to boast of our position [as Christians] we should remember that we are but Gentiles, while the Jews are of the lineage of Christ. We are aliens and in-laws; they are blood relatives, cousins, and brothers of our Lord. Therefore, if one is to boast of flesh and blood the Jews are actually nearer to Christ than we are... If we really want to help them, we must be guided in our dealings with them not by papal law but by the law of Christian love... If some of them should prove stiff-necked, what of it? After all, we ourselves are not all good Christians either.[6]

The question of whether Luther was really an anti-Semite, and if so to what degree and in what way, is hotly debated today. Nevertheless, one thing is clear from Luther's attitude to Judaism, which he shared with Chrysostom as well as with Augustine and the other ancient exclusivists: whatever the historical role of the Jews in God's plan of salvation, Judaism since Christ has been a false path. It is no more a route to salvation than classical paganism is.

This is the classical exclusivist position, and it finds some support in the New Testament too. The twentieth chapter of Revelation speaks of the 'bottomless pit' and the 'lake of fire', noting that 'whoever was not found written in the book of life was cast into the lake of fire'. Luke 16:19–31 tells the story of the rich man and the beggar Lazarus: after their deaths, Lazarus enjoys a feast with Abraham, while the rich man is tormented in hell, apparently without the prospect of respite. Matthew 5:22, 30 and similar verses speak of 'Gehenna'. Strikingly, all these passages suggest that damnation, when it comes, comes about because people fail to act morally – not because of their religious beliefs. This is a view endorsed by Matthew 25:31–46, the story of the sheep and the goats, where we are told that it is those who failed to feed the hungry, clothe the naked and visit the imprisoned who are damned.

More support for exclusivism can be found in a number of other passages, such as Acts 4:12, where Peter is represented as saying 'Neither is there salvation in any other [than Christ]: for there is none other name under heaven given among men, whereby we must be saved.' Several passages like this also come in John's Gospel. For example, after describing himself as the True Vine, Jesus says:

> Whoever does not abide in me is thrown away like a branch and withers; such branches are gathered, thrown into the fire, and burned.
> **John 15:6**

And in John 14:6, Jesus declares, 'I am the way, the truth, and the life. No one comes to the Father except by me.' Most stark of all, we have this:

> Those who believe in him are not condemned; but those who do not believe are condemned already, because they have not believed in the name of the only Son of God.
> **John 3:18**

However, virtually all of the texts and authors we have looked at here are speaking only of those who *deliberately* reject Christianity (whether because they are heretics, schismatics, or follow another religion entirely). For example, the great scholar Jerome wrote:

> Heretics bring sentence upon themselves since they by their own choice withdraw from the church, a withdrawal which, since they are aware of it, constitutes damnation. Between heresy and schism there is this difference: that heresy involves perverse doctrine, while schism separates one from the church on account of disagreement with the bishop. Nevertheless, there is no schism which does not trump up a heresy to justify its departure from the Church.[7]

The Church Fathers hardly had to deal with the notion of people who had simply never heard of Christianity. Still, there is no problem, at least in principle, of extending the idea here too. Augustine wrote that unbaptized babies are condemned to hell – and justly, too – because they share in Adam's guilt. This is so even though the babies have obviously not had a chance to accept or reject Christ (Augustine did allow, on this basis, that they suffer only the lightest kind of hellfire). The same principle would presumably apply to adults who live in distant countries and have never heard the Christian message.

And this is exactly what happened. Augustine's influence upon the church – at least, upon the Western church – was so great that this became the standard view. In the Middle Ages, it was not really possible to doubt exclusivism. One of the Christian writers who came closest to it was Julian of Norwich. In chapter 3 we saw how she struggled with the problem of evil, and in her eyes, one of the biggest elements of the problem of evil was the fact of damnation. She stated that really she did not want to believe in such a thing, although the authority of the church told her that it must be true; the problem of evil, for her, was thus the fact that so many people will ultimately be damned. The exclusivist attitude was one of the major motivations behind the explosion in missionary activity that occurred in the sixteenth and seventeenth centuries on the part of Western Christians – for if non-Christians must necessarily be condemned, the principle of charity demands that they must be converted if at all possible. Thus we read of the sheer hatred that many missionaries felt towards the indigenous religions of the people to whom they preached in other continents. Francis Xavier, for example, the greatest missionary of the sixteenth century, wrote a letter in 1545 about his activities in India:

> When I have finished baptising the people, I order them to destroy the huts in which they keep their idols; and I have them break the statues of their idols into tiny pieces, since they are now Christians. I could never come to an end describing to you the great consolation which fills my soul when I see idols being destroyed by the hands of those who had been idolaters.[8]

It was the same story in Africa, where most missionaries condemned the indigenous religions as 'fetishism'. Conversion was invariably accompanied by a demand that the 'fetishes' be destroyed, and many missionaries were bemused and discouraged by the reluctance on the part of some converts to do this. Luca da Caltanisetta, a Sicilian Capuchin friar who worked in Congo in the 1690s, wrote in his journal:

> At Mbanza Zolu I sent word to the king to tell the fetishists to stop their dances and these diabolic ceremonies. They replied that they could not stop. Then I said he had to catch them and chain them or else I would come myself and catch them... I beat the heads of two idols one against the other and threw them into the fire. At that, these ignorant people showed their sadness and defiance, and almost in tears with depression they withdrew, not wishing to see their filth being burned.[9]

Unrealized Inclusivism

Yet if exclusivism has been the dominant view in Western Christianity, it has often been accompanied by its counterpart, inclusivism. Indeed, both views can sometimes be found in the same author.

'Inclusivism' is a much-used term, as a result of which it has become quite ambiguous. The sense in which I'm using it here is therefore not necessarily definitive, but I think it is the most helpful one. Broadly, 'inclusivism' means the belief that salvation can be found outside the church – but still through Christ only, in some sense. There are two main versions of this belief. It's not always recognized that this is the case, since even inclusivists themselves have, historically, been rather bad at distinguishing them. Here, I shall treat them separately.

The first version of this belief revolves around eschatology and, in particular, the notion that human beings can still make significant choices even in the next life. If this is so, then it is possible that those who die unconverted and unrepentant may change their minds after death. It is even possible that *everyone* will do so. I shall call this view 'unrealized inclusivism', since it suggests that salvation *will* be available to all people; it is not available yet. It could just as easily be regarded as a form of exclusivism: as we have seen, exclusivists hold that only Christians can be saved, and unrealized inclusivists agree with this. They differ only in that they hold that even those who die outside the faith still have the chance to become Christians. And many (though not all) unrealized inclusivists hold that *everyone* will, ultimately, become a Christian.

The architect of unrealized inclusivism was Origen. Origen's views on this matter are among the hardest to reconstruct of all his beliefs, since they are controversial, and they even seem to have got him into some trouble during his lifetime. He could write passages that sound as exclusivist as anything in Augustine:

> Outside of the church, no one is saved; for, if anyone should go out of it, he is guilty of his own death.[10]

However, Origen seems to have combined this attitude with the apparently contradictory one that everyone would be saved:

> There is a resurrection of the dead, and there is punishment, but not everlasting. For when the body is punished the soul is gradually purified, and so is restored to its ancient rank. For all wicked men, and for demons, too, punishment has an end, and both wicked men and demons shall be restored to their former rank.[11]

Origen accepted the Stoic belief in a succession of universes: when this world comes to an end, there will be another one, and we will all be reincarnated in it. But where the Stoics thought that each world would be identical to the preceding one, in an eternity of repetition, Origen thought that people would retain freedom of choice in each world. In each lifetime, we will have the opportunity to come closer to God. Often, no doubt, people will choose to fall further from God. But that can't go on for ever, because there is a limit to how evil it is possible to become – for, in Origen's view, evil is simply a lack of good. Ultimately, everyone will choose to turn to God in Christ. Thus, Origen can reconcile his (apparent) belief in the salvation of everyone with his insistence that the church is the only vehicle of salvation: despite appearances, everyone will join the church, even if not in this life.

Origen's doctrine may seem to be sustainable only if one accepts a number of potentially rather shocking theses, such as the succession of worlds and reincarnation. But a number of other Christians of his period seem to have shared his universalism whilst retaining a more orthodox understanding of history. Gregory of Nyssa, for example, wrote repeatedly that all people would be saved, without subscribing to Origen's cyclical understanding of history. Like Origen, Gregory believed that hell is only temporary, since it is essentially purgatorial in nature. Even those in hell always retain the option of turning to God; and, given an infinite amount of time, as well as the infinite goodness of God, all of them eventually will. Similar, though less clearly worked out, views can be found in Clement of Alexandria, Titus of Bostra and other luminaries of the third and fourth centuries. Interestingly, the view was somewhat controversial, but not very much. Gregory of Nyssa, in particular, never gives any indication that he regards his own universalism as something unusual; he just mentions it in passing. His own brother, Basil of Caesarea, did attack the doctrine, while their mutual friend Gregory of Nazianzus wasn't sure which one to believe.

Clearly, this doctrine is compatible with the various verses of the New Testament, mentioned above, that suggest that salvation can be found only through Christ. Unrealized inclusivists are not committed to denying that doctrine. Rather, they distinguish between those who follow Christ *now* and those who will do so *ultimately*.

From a historical point of view, inclusivism was more or less killed off by Augustine, who devoted much of the twenty-first book of *City of God* to arguing against it. He suggested that those who believe that all people will be saved might as well extend salvation to the demons, and even to Satan himself. He evidently regarded this as a sort of *reductio ad absurdum* – clearly it's ridiculous to suggest that Satan will be saved, so it would be equally ridiculous to suppose that all human beings will. In fact, Origen was accused in his own lifetime of believing that Satan would be saved. He insisted that he did not teach this, although it is possible that in fact he did; certainly Augustine was right to see this as the logical consequence of Origen's views on human salvation. Augustine also attacked those who (like Origen and Gregory of Nyssa) argued that the punishment of hell would be only temporary. Augustine pointed out that the New Testament uses the word 'eternal' to refer to both the bliss of the saved and the anguish of the damned; if the latter were only temporary, then the former would be too. In this, at least, Augustine's poor grasp of Greek let him down. The Greek word used in passages such as Matthew 25:46 for 'eternal' (*ainios*) simply means 'for a very long time', so it could be used for periods that are not everlasting. And indeed it is used elsewhere in the New Testament to describe long, but limited, periods of time, such as in 1 Corinthians 10:11. In fact the word is best translated as something like 'of the ages'; it is often used by other classical writers to mean *this* age – that is, life as we know it. The vagueness of the term means that Augustine shouldn't really have tried to use it as the basis of a definite doctrine of the eternity of punishment.

Realized Inclusivism

An alternative version of inclusivism was also put forward in the early centuries of Christianity. Rather than accept the exclusivist thesis that only Christians can be saved, but then suggest that ultimately everyone will become a Christian, proponents of this view distinguished between being a Christian and having faith in Christ. The idea is that Christ can be found in other religions or even among people with none. So I shall call it 'realized inclusivism', because it suggests that Christ and salvation are available to people who are not Christians, *right now*. In this view, it is not the case that people (even the dead) must wait until they become Christians before they can know Christ; it is possible even for people who have never heard of Christianity.

The godfather of this approach was Justin Martyr. He described Christ himself as the *Logos*, that is, the Reason of God. Christ is, literally, God's rational faculty (though he is more than that too, of course). The title '*Logos*' is applied to Christ in the first chapter of John, but Justin extended the thought. The Stoics also believed that God has a reason, and they suggested that the reason of each individual person is a sort of fragment of this divine reason. Thus, to follow our reason – to behave rationally – is, in a way, to put ourselves in touch with the divine. Justin incorporated this idea into his Christian philosophy. He concluded:

> We have been taught that Christ is the first-born of God, and we have declared above that he is the Logos of whom every race of men were partakers. And those who lived according to reason [*Logos*] are Christians, even though they have been thought atheists; as, among the Greeks, Socrates and Heraclitus, and men like them; and among the barbarians, Abraham, and Ananias, and Azarias, and Misael, and Elias, and many others whose actions and names we now decline to recount, because we know it would be tedious.[12]

In this view, then, those who are not Christians may actually be following Christ without knowing it. Despite the fame of this passage, Justin does not say much else on this subject or develop the idea further – at least, not in his writings that survive.

Realized inclusivism seems to have been much less popular among the early Christians than unrealized inclusivism. Whatever traces of it remained by the time of Augustine were largely killed off together with unrealized inclusivism, following the success of his arguments for exclusivism. We have already seen that unrealized inclusivism is quite compatible with the biblical verses apparently endorsing exclusivism. It is worth pointing out that the same is true of realized exclusivism. Those verses all speak of the necessity of *Christ* for salvation – not of the necessity of consciously following the Christian religion.

We have already seen how exclusivism dominated most traditions of Christianity after this point. In modern times, however, realized inclusivism has become much more popular again. The edifice of exclusivism began to crack in early modern times when missionaries and other explorers reached foreign, advanced cultures and were impressed by their religious or moral ideals. The eighteenth century, for example, saw a boom of interest in Chinese philosophy and religion among European intellectuals. The German philosopher Christian Wolff was expelled from Prussia for his statement that Chinese sages such as Confucius had expressed moral truths without needing divine revelation; this incident reflects both the new kinds of views that were emerging and the reaction against them.

Inclusivism made a real comeback, however, in the twentieth century. Two of the most important Christian writers of the century, Karl Barth and Karl Rahner, advocated the two different versions of it. Often misidentified as an exclusivist, Barth, without doubt the most influential theologian of the twentieth century, seems in fact to have been an unrealized inclusivist, like Origen. He insisted that salvation can come only through an explicit act of faith in Christ, but he believed that God's grace would ultimately triumph and bring everyone to make such an act (in the next life if not in this).

Rahner, meanwhile, was a realized inclusivist, like Justin Martyr. He argued that it is inconsistent to say, on the one hand, that God wishes everyone to be saved, and insist, on the other, that salvation is available only to those who have lived at certain times and places in history. After all, innumerable people lived before Jesus and never had the chance to hear about him; and since then, many more people have lived in cultures where the gospel has not yet reached. Would it be just for God to condemn them all?

It is senseless to suppose cruelly – and without any hope of acceptance by the man of today, in view of the enormous extent of the extra-Christian history of salvation and damnation – that nearly all men living outside the official and public Christianity are so evil and stubborn that the offer of supernatural grace ought not even to be made in fact in most cases, since these individuals have already rendered themselves unworthy of such an offer by previous, subjectively grave offences against the natural moral law.[13]

Rahner distinguishes between Christianity (a historical religion, which originated at a particular point in time and in a particular place, and has enjoyed various successes and suffered various defeats since then) and the means to salvation through Christ (something universal and eternal, since it comes from the universal and eternal divine will to save). Historically, Christians have tended to identify the two. On that view – the exclusivist view – salvation has been possible only where Christianity has existed. Moreover, when Christianity first appeared – say, on the day of Pentecost in Jerusalem – on that day, being a Christian became necessary to salvation for every person in the entire world. In place of this, Rahner suggests that we date the appearance of Christianity (and therefore the necessity of being a Christian for salvation) in different cultures to different times.

In other words, Rahner agrees with the exclusivists that, once you have encountered Christianity and truly understood it, becoming a Christian is essential if you are to be saved. But the point at which this situation is reached is different for different groups and individuals. In 1513, for example, the Spanish authorities introduced the notorious *Requirement*, a statement which all Spanish explorers in the New World had to read to all native peoples they encountered. The *Requirement* was a brief explanation of Christianity and a demand that the natives submit to the Spanish crown. Since it was invariably read out in Spanish or Latin, the uncomprehending natives always ended up being simply conquered by force. Now, technically, these natives had had the gospel preached to them, but clearly not in a way that could be understood. For Rahner, they were still in the same state that, say, the Jews were in before Pentecost. And we could extend this idea further. Today, in the West, there are many people who, despite coming from traditionally Christian countries, know virtually nothing of what Christians actually believe. Perhaps we could say the same of them. In Rahner's view, it is only when 'Christianity reaches man in the real urgency and rigour of his actual existence' that it becomes a live option, that someone must choose for or against Christ. Yet how many people are really in such a position?

If, then, more people are in a pre-Pentecost state than traditional exclusivists have been prepared to admit, what happens to them if they never do hear or understand the Christian message? Rahner suggests that Christ can be present in other religions, even if their adherents don't realize it:

> However little we can say with certitude about the final lot of an individual inside or outside the officially constituted Christian religion, we have every reason to think optimistically – i.e., truly hopefully and confidently in a Christian sense – of God who has certainly the last word and who has revealed to us that he has spoken his powerful word of reconciliation and forgiveness into the world… Once we take all this into consideration, we will not hold it to be impossible that grace is at work, and is even being accepted, in the spiritual, personal life of the individual, no matter how primitive, unenlightened, apathetic and earth-bound such a life may at first sight seem to be… Hence, if one believes seriously in the universal salvific purpose of God towards all men in Christ, it need not and cannot really be doubted that gratuitous influences of properly Christian supernatural grace are conceivable in the life of all men (provided they are first of all regarded as individuals) and that these influences can be presumed to be accepted in spite of the sinful state of men and in spite of their apparent estrangement from God.[14]

Rahner coined the term 'anonymous Christians' to refer to such people. But like Justin before him, Rahner stressed that Christ is present within Christianity to a far greater degree than in other religions, so other religions are not equal to Christianity. There is much in other religions that is wrong or hinders their adherents from finding God. Following another religion is rather like going to a concert by a tribute band – no one would do that if they had the opportunity to go to a concert by the originals, but it is a lot better than nothing. Once the Pentecost moment has been reached for any group or individual, Christianity becomes essential for their salvation – for how could anyone claim to be following Christian principles in their own way if they rejected Christianity itself?

Rahner's theory has attracted a lot of criticism, partly from exclusivists who regard it as a watering down of the gospel, but partly from pluralists (more on them in a moment) who accuse it of patronizing arrogance. Who is Rahner – or anyone else – to tell adherents of other religions that they are really Christians even if they don't know it? The force of this objection is questionable, however. Rahner didn't propose that Christians go around telling people of other faiths that they are really Christians; rather, he suggested the idea as a doctrine for Christians themselves. In particular, it is intended as a sort of pastoral response to the question asked by many Christians: how can a loving God send people to hell simply because they have never heard of Jesus? It is, in effect, a sort of theodicy, not a basis for ecumenical dialogue. Besides which, of course, whether a doctrine is arrogant or patronizing or not really doesn't have much effect on whether it is *true*. Should Christians, or anyone else, seek to believe only what is inoffensive or desirable, rather than what is actually the case?

Something like Rahner's view has become quite mainstream within Catholicism. In the 1960s, the Second Vatican Council (at which Rahner was an important theological adviser) made the following statement:

Those also can attain to salvation who through no fault of their own do not know the Gospel of Christ or His Church, yet sincerely seek God and moved by grace strive by their deeds to do His will as it is known to them through the dictates of conscience. Nor does Divine Providence deny the helps necessary for salvation to those who, without blame on their part, have not yet arrived at an explicit knowledge of God and with His grace strive to live a good life. Whatever good or truth is found amongst them is looked upon by the Church as a preparation for the Gospel.[15]

In 2000, Joseph Ratzinger (the future Pope Benedict XVI) issued a document called *Domine Iesus*, in which he suggested that other religions do contain truth, and their prayers, rituals and so on may contain elements that help their adherents draw closer to salvation. However, salvation comes only through Christ, and Christ is present in his fullness only in the Christian church. There is much in non-Christian religions to hinder their adherents as well as to help them. Here, then, we see moderate inclusivism tempered by an overriding stress on the incompleteness of Christ's revelation and presence in non-Christian religions.

Pluralism

The fourth major approach that Christians have taken to other religions is usually known as pluralism: the belief that different religions offer different routes to God and to salvation, and that no one religion (either Christianity or any other) should claim any kind of exclusivity.

It is important to clarify this belief at the outset. Being a pluralist doesn't necessarily commit someone to the view that all religions are *equally* true. That is certainly a fairly widespread belief. In one episode of *The Simpsons*, the long-suffering Reverend Lovejoy, sick of the constant questions from one over-anxious member of his congregation, asks him, 'Ned, have you considered any of the other major religions? They're all pretty much the same.' Of course the joke is that a Christian minister should say such a thing, but many people do think this. Nevertheless, although there are clearly similarities between many religions, there are also quite fundamental differences. Not all religions feature God; of those that do, they disagree about what he is like. Different religions also have different rituals and different ecclesiastical hierarchies, and they teach different ethical systems. It is hard, for example, to see much in common between Islam and Shinto. Although we should not downplay the similarities between different religions, we should also not allow them to blind us to the equally real differences.

Pluralism, in the sense that we are using the word here, also does not commit someone to the even more extreme view that everything is true, or that nothing is true, or that 'truth' is an outdated concept at all. Views like this are sometimes called 'relativism', a very vague term. Many pluralists are relativists, at least in some sense of that word, but by no means all.

It is also important to distinguish pluralism in the sense defined above from pluralism in the sense of the co-existence of different cultures. It is often said that many people today live in a pluralistic society, meaning that people of different cultures live side by side. That is simply a fact about life – and, as we see from the story of William of Rubruck at the court of the Great Khan, it has been a fact of life for many people for a long time. Pluralism in the sense given above, however, is an attitude or belief that is in part inspired by this fact. Pluralists in this sense do not simply seek to get on with those of other faiths; they believe that these other faiths offer routes to truth that are quite different from their own, but which are nevertheless valid. One image that has sometimes been used is that of a globe, with many people trying to travel from the south pole to the north pole. There are many different routes that one could take from one to the other, but the final goal is the same.

Historically, pluralism has been very much the minority view in Christianity. One striking early exception occurred in India. There was a thriving Christian church there, in what is now the state of Kerala, from at least the fourth or fifth century AD (later traditions credit the apostle Thomas with bringing Christianity there in the first century). The Christian Indians apparently did well for themselves (helped, in part, by a reputation for honesty – most customs officers were Christians), and many lived as high-caste members of Hindu society, riding elephants, sitting on rich carpets and practising traditional Hindu customs such as the separation of the sexes. And they seem to have adopted the typical Hindu attitude to other religions, which is to consider them all valid routes to the truth. To a Hindu, each religion has its own *dharma* – a way of life or path to God. The Indian Christians seem to have shared this view. They believed that Hindus, for example, could be saved by following their own religion sincerely. And they did not base this belief on a conviction, like that of Justin Martyr, that Christ could be found in religions outside Christianity, but upon the conviction that even a Christless religion could have an alternative, equally valid grasp of the truth.

This attitude was endorsed by another great Indian religious teacher, the Buddha. In a famous parable, the Buddha likened bickering religious teachers to blind men examining an elephant. Each blind man touches a different part of the elephant and insists that the elephant is like a pot, a plough, a brush and so on, depending on which part they have touched. As they argue, they fail to realize that each one is right in his own way, but none of them has the whole picture.

In modern times, pluralism has become much more popular within Christianity. One of the major proponents of this view is the English theologian John Hick. At first a traditionally-minded exclusivist, Hick became dissatisfied with this position when he came into contact with people of different faiths and attended their religious services. It was apparent that Muslims, Hindus and others lived just as morally as Christians and that their rituals were not so different from Christian ones. So how could Christians be justified in claiming some kind of moral and metaphysical superiority over them? Hick has therefore called for a 'Copernican revolution' in religious thought. Copernicus, of course, argued that instead of the sun and everything else revolving around the earth, it was actually the earth that revolved around the sun. Similarly, as Hick presents it, Christian exclusivists and inclusivists alike have traditionally made other religions revolve around Christianity. For them, Christianity is the only true religion, and the other religions are to be evaluated according to how to close to this one truth they come. Instead, Hick suggests that we see Christianity as just one faith among others, all of which are trying to get close to 'Reality':

> Each of the great religious traditions affirms that in addition to the social and natural world of our ordinary human experience there is a limitlessly greater and higher Reality beyond or within us, in relation to which or to whom is our greatest good. The ultimately real and the ultimately valuable are one, and to give oneself freely and totally to this One is our final salvation/liberation/enlightenment/fulfilment. Further, each tradition is conscious that the divine Reality exceeds the reach of our earthly speech and thought. It cannot be encompassed in human concepts. It is infinite, eternal, limitlessly rich beyond the scope of our finite conceiving or experiencing.[16]

Clearly, different religions offer different conceptions of this 'Reality'. Some call it God, some use a different name. Some believe that this Reality is personal, others that it is not. Even among theistic religions, there are differences: Christians believe that God is a Trinity, while Muslims do not. So how can they all be worshipping the same thing? Hick's answer is much the same as the Buddha's. There is a difference between perception and reality. Each religion's portrait of Reality is an authentic expression of how this Reality seems to adherents of that religion, but it is necessarily partial. It is just like a group of people looking at the world through tinted spectacles of different colours. Each one will perceive the world in a different way – one will think it is pink, another green and so on – and they may have bitter arguments about what colour it really is. But they are all looking at the same world, and they are all really seeing it, though in a distorted way.

Hick's views have been extremely influential. Many Christians have felt that this sort of approach better reflects the pluralistic world in which we live – one in which members of different faiths not only live shoulder-to-shoulder but must interact and respect each other. Can that realistically be done if each person assumes that those of different traditions are necessarily completely wrong (and probably damned to hell)? Thus we find that pluralistic views are not confined only to the liberal wing of Christianity today, but members of other Christian traditions are often attracted to them. For example, George W. Bush – normally branded a reactionary in his religious views – has expressed in some interviews a belief that different religions offer independent routes to God. But he has, at other times, also expressed the view that certain religions (such as Wicca) are intrinsically inferior to others, which may indicate that a *tendency* to pluralism does not necessarily translate into a wholehearted *acceptance* of it.

The popularity of pluralism also reflects the increasing sense that no one religion has a monopoly on sainthood. As Hick points out, if only one religion were true, you'd expect its history to be packed with great and good deeds, and many enlightened teachers, while the other religions would have virtually none. But in fact this is not the case, and each religion can claim both great saints and great sinners.

Others have been less enthusiastic. Hick-style pluralism seems incompatible with a conservative theological outlook; for example, accepting it involves also accepting that the 'exclusivist' verses of the New Testament mentioned earlier are simply wrong. So those unhappy with theological liberalism will be equally unhappy with pluralism.

Another common criticism is that no one can seriously claim that *all* religions are equally true or valid. Surely some kind of ghastly satanic cult shouldn't be viewed as equal in value to Buddhism or Christianity. However, as I suggested above, pluralists are not necessarily committed to such a view. Hick certainly is not, and indeed he offers criteria by which we can rank religions and judge how valid their claim to offer a path to truth really is. He talks, for example, of 'Reality' and suggests that what really matters in each religion is the way in which it offers a route to salvation (its 'soteriological efficacy'):

> These many different perceptions of the Real, both theistic and nontheistic, can only establish themselves as authentic by their soteriological efficacy. The great world traditions have in fact all proved to be realms within which or routes along which people are enabled to advance in the transition from self-centredness to Reality-centredness. And, since they reveal the Real in such different lights, we must conclude that they are independently valid.[17]

Thus, a child-murdering cult of devil-worshippers would fail this test. But this does open Hick up to another criticism that is sometimes made, which is that by ranking religions in this way he ends up smuggling in the very Christian judgmentalism that his theory is meant to avoid. His 'Reality', for example, sounds like just a new name for 'God'; and the centrality of salvation (conceived in terms of selflessness) as a concern of religion sounds very Christian. Some other religions are more concerned with things other than salvation, and some (such as Shinto, for example) aren't particularly bothered about salvation at all. And a Muslim pluralist, say, might rank religions in a very different way, perhaps according to how much they encourage believers to submit to the will of 'Reality'. So it looks like Hick is really judging other religions by the criteria of Christianity after all. Perhaps there is nothing wrong with that – but if it is true, then his pluralism really collapses into a sort of realized inclusivism, of the kind that he explicitly wishes to avoid.

Pluralism and Speaking about God
Perhaps more fundamentally, though, pluralism raises questions about the nature of religious claims. On the face of it, religious believers make claims about reality which seem plainly factual. Thus, if a Christian says that God is three persons in one substance,

this seems to be a factual claim (irrespective of whether it is right or wrong). The same is true when a Muslim says that Allah is one. It looks as if at least one of them must be wrong, since their claims contradict each other. It is as if one person said that the world was round and another said it was flat; they cannot both be right. So for pluralism to be viable, religious claims would have to function in a different way. The claims of the Christian and the Muslim may *look* like simple factual claims – just like those of the round-earther and the flat-earther – but in fact they are not.

How could this work? In fact, the nature of religious language is not only a major issue in modern philosophy of religion, but has been debated within Christianity for much longer than pluralism has been. As we saw in chapter 1, there has always been a strong tradition within Christianity of emphasizing the unknowability of God. But if God transcends all comprehensible categories, how can we talk about him at all? One solution was that of Gregory of Nyssa. According to him, the name 'God' and its cognates actually refer to our experiences of God, that is, his action. They don't refer to God as he is in himself. A view like this could be combined quite nicely with pluralism: perhaps members of different religions are simply referring to different actions or experiences of the divinity. Thus it could be true both that God is a Trinity and that Allah is indivisibly one, because 'God' and 'Allah' here simply refer to different experiences of one underlying and inexpressible reality. A difficulty with this theory is that it implies that no one ever talks about God at all, which seems problematic from a religious point of view.

A more developed theory, with similarities to that of Gregory, was put forward by the enormously influential German theologian Friedrich Schleiermacher in the nineteenth century. As we saw in chapter 5, Schleiermacher argued that religion is basically 'about' experience – in particular, the experience of being dependent upon God. In the case of Christianity, it revolves around the experience of being saved by God through Christ. All doctrines are simply attempts to articulate this feeling. So the Christian doctrine of the Trinity, for example, is not simply 'about' God. It is an attempt to express God *as he is experienced* by the believer.

Yet another variant on this approach is that of Thomas Hobbes.

According to him, most language about God is actually honorific. It expresses how God is to be honoured, or perhaps how we actually do honour God, rather than what God is like in himself:

> And therefore, when men out of the principles of natural reason dispute of the attributes of God, they but dishonour him; for in the attributes which we give to God, we are not to consider the signification of philosophical truth, but the signification of pious intention to do him the greatest honour we are able.[18]

Hobbes thinks that some statements about God are literally true – such as the claim that he exists, or that he is the cause of the world – but most are really practical statements about what attitude we should have towards him. As such, they are not descriptive at all, even though they may seem to be.

With views like these, one could easily interpret the doctrines of different religions as different attempts to express either similar experiences or different experiences of the same underlying reality, or as different attitudes of the kind of honour appropriate to God. They are not really true or false, any more than 'Ouch!' is true or false or an act of obeisance is true or false. So they can't really contradict each other.

An alternative approach was that of Thomas Aquinas, who argued that all language about God is really analogy. So when we say that God is loving, we don't mean that he experiences love in the same sense that we do. We mean that he has a quality which is somehow *like* love as we know it, but still very different. This theory of analogy was powerfully attacked by Aquinas' critic John Duns Scotus, who pointed out that if the divine love has nothing whatsoever in common with human love then we might as well not call it 'love' at all. But on the other hand, if the divine love *is* in some way similar to human love, then there must be some quality which both genuinely share – in which case, we can attribute human qualities to God in a non-analogous way after all. Nevertheless, the theory of analogy has many defenders today, and it too could be combined well with a pluralistic outlook. If all language about God is analogous, then none of it is literally true; so two statements about God that seem to contradict each other might not do so after all.

Hick himself has appealed to the category of 'mythical truth' as distinct from 'literal truth'. A claim is mythologically true if it is literally false *but* has the effect of creating the right attitude in those who hear it. An example might be the story of Adam and Eve and the fall of humanity. According to Hick, this is literally false (it never really happened) but it has religious value in that it encourages those who hear it to consider how they have fallen short of God's standards and to desire salvation. Thus, it is mythologically true. In his analysis of myth, Hick is not alone. Although in the nineteenth century many theologians dismissed traditional myths as simply false and not worth bothering with, the twentieth century saw theologians typically more sensitive to the value of myths even where they are not literally true.

Salvation of All?

Choosing between exclusivism, inclusivism and pluralism is made all the harder by the additional complication of universalism. Universalism is simply the belief that everyone will be saved. We have already seen this belief crop up throughout this chapter, mainly in connection with inclusivism, but it is important to recognize that it is not identical with either inclusivism or pluralism. It's clearly not even compatible with exclusivism, at least as we have defined it above. It does seem to be implied by unrealized inclusivism, of the kind defended by Origen and Gregory of Nyssa: if, ultimately, all creatures turn to Christ, then all creatures will be saved. Realized inclusivism, however, needn't entail universalism. One could believe that Christ can be found in other religions without also believing that everyone *actually* finds Christ in their religion. Perhaps a good Muslim is following Christ without knowing it, but a bad Muslim might not be following Christ at all. The same goes for pluralism. Perhaps many or even all religions offer alternative and valid routes to God, but it doesn't follow from this that their adherents all follow those routes. And what about people who aren't religious at all? Some pluralists may argue that you don't have to be religious at all – perhaps it's enough to be a good person. But what about the people who aren't good in any sense?

Christians have certainly disagreed over whether universalism is an acceptable doctrine at all. Despite the minority of Christians who seem to have believed it fairly uncontroversially in late antiquity, it was later regarded as a heresy. It was condemned at Constantinople in AD 543. However, it reappeared in early modern times and became popular among a number of Christian intellectuals in the eighteenth century. At this time, it was often associated with unitarianism – the denial of the Trinity – and many people who believed in one believed in the other. For example, Joseph Priestly, the British chemist who preached unitarianism in America, was also a universalist, while Hosea Ballou, the American universalist who was very influential in the early nineteenth century, was also a unitarian. Today, universalist tendencies (at least) are extremely widespread among theologians, though less so among other Christians. As we have seen, the texts often used to support exclusivism do not seem to rule out either form of inclusivism. I think that unrealized inclusivism is especially easy to reconcile with these texts, since it does not even depend upon distinguishing between those who follow Christ and those who follow the Christian religion (as realized inclusivism does). Those who wish to defend universalism – whether through pluralism or some form of inclusivism – can point to texts of their own. The one most commonly cited is this:

For as in Adam all die, so also in Christ shall all be made alive. But each in his own order: Christ the first fruits, then at his coming those who belong to Christ. Then comes the end, when he delivers the kingdom to God the Father after destroying every rule and every authority and power. For he must reign until he has put all his enemies under his feet. The last enemy to be destroyed is death. 'For God has put all things in subjection under his feet.'... When all things are subjected to him, then the Son himself will also be subjected to him who put all things under him, that God may everything to everybody.
1 Corinthians 15:24–28

The last rather cryptic phrase is also often translated 'that God may be all in all', which is equally hard to understand beyond the fact that it will apparently apply to *everybody*. In fact the Greek here – *pantos* – means every*thing*, not just every*body*. Equally striking, though, is Paul's statement at the start of the passage that everyone will be made alive in Christ, just as everyone died in Adam. The idea that Christ is a second Adam is an important one in Paul's theology, and it is true that if the parallelism is to be observed exactly, and if the sin and suffering brought by Adam is universal (which Paul thinks it is), then so too the salvation brought by Christ ought to be universal. As he writes elsewhere:

> Then as one man's trespass led to condemnation for all men, so one man's act of righteousness leads to acquittal and life for all men. For as by one man's disobedience many were made sinners, so by one man's obedience many will be made righteous.
> **Romans 5:18–19**

These passages suggest, then, that a tendency towards universalism can be found in the New Testament. Given the passages we have already seen insisting on the necessity of faith in Christ for salvation, it seems that inclusivism – of either variety – might seem to be more in keeping with the New Testament than either exclusivism or pluralism.

Chapter 9

What Does it Mean to Lead a Good Life?

What makes a good act good, or a bad act bad? Such a simple question – but it has been perhaps debated more than any other in history, from the time of the ancient Greeks to today. There now exists a bewildering array of possible responses for the curious to choose between. Has there been any distinctive Christian response to the problem?

It may be surprising to find that here – as in other matters – Christians have disagreed with each other quite profoundly. Surely part of the *raison d'être* of Christianity is to help people live their lives – surely this should be a point of basic agreement between Christians at least? Part of the problem here is that ethics is really part of the domain of philosophy. That doesn't prevent Christians from commenting on it, of course, but it does mean that certain claims about ethics will commit those who make them to other, perhaps undesirable, philosophical points of view.

A Matter of Motive

One of the most important points that Christian writers have made about ethics is the significance of motive. Normally, we distinguish between an act itself and the reason why we perform it. This distinction was also recognized by ancient moralists. Aristotle believed that being virtuous isn't simply a matter of behaving in a certain way; it is to behave in a certain way *for a particular reason*. In his view, the emotions play a major role in ethics. It is better to be virtuous in a happy way, because you enjoy it, than it is to be virtuous out of some miserable, grudging sense of duty. And that is why parents try to bring up their children to *want* to be good. We find a similar concern in Matthew 5–6, Jesus' famous Sermon on the Mount. Here, Jesus is represented as teaching his disciples that it's not enough to act in the right way – you have to be the right sort of person on the 'inside', too:

> You have learned that our forefathers were told, 'Do not commit murder; anyone who commits murder must be brought to judgment.' But what I tell you is this: anyone who nurses anger against his brother must be brought to judgment… You have learned that they were told, 'Do not commit adultery.' But what I tell you is this: if a man looks on a woman with a lustful eye, he has already committed adultery with her in his heart.
> **Matthew 5:21–28**

It's not entirely clear what the reasoning is here; after all, it's all very well to talk of committing adultery in your heart, but that is still not the same thing as doing it for real, and we are not explicitly told *why* it is a bad thing. Presumably the idea is partly like Aristotle's: being a good person is a matter of wanting what is good, not simply doing it. And that is partly because someone who does not want what is good is less likely to do it. Perhaps someone who spends time nursing lustful thoughts is more likely to end up committing adultery for real.

So according to the Sermon on the Mount, simply not performing wrong actions is not sufficient for someone to count as being good. Acting properly, but with the wrong desires, will not do. Jesus tells his listeners to 'be perfect' (Matthew 5:48), and the idea seems to be that perfection extends to the inner life as well as the outer. It must be admitted that this notion is not consistently taught in the New Testament. In Romans 12:20, Paul suggests that behaving nicely to one's enemies will result in God heaping coals on their heads in the future – a use of hatred to motivate moral behaviour. Of course, Paul was also capable of the reverse sentiments; in Romans 9:3 he expresses the wish that he could be damned if it would save the Jews, surely as selfless a remark as one could hope for. And in Romans 13:9

he instructs his readers to love others as themselves, without any apparent restriction on who should be the recipients of this love. Rather than presenting a unified theory of morality, Paul is normally content simply to present his readers with lists of virtues and vices (generally fairly standard lists, from the viewpoint of first-century Judaism) and use whatever ad hoc arguments occur to him to persuade his readers to be virtuous.

The first really thorough attempt at a Christian system of morality – and one which was also the first to put an emphasis on the importance of motive – was that of Augustine. In one of his earliest works, *On Free Will*, written shortly after his conversion to Christianity, Augustine argues that sin and evil come about purely as a result of the actions of free creatures. We saw in chapter 3 how this forms a major part of Augustine's attempt to reconcile the goodness of God with the existence of evil. But it also has important ramifications for both his ethics and his psychology. In fact, it has often been said that Augustine invented, virtually single-handedly, the modern notion of the will, conceived as a faculty of the soul analogous to the understanding, the ability to desire and other faculties. It is by the operation of this will that we perform actions that can truly be said to be our own. Augustine believes that evil is to be found only in this will, which is the cause of all sinful actions. Therefore, morality is a matter not of what we actually do, but of what we will to do.

This notion seems both to agree with and to contradict how we normally think. On the one hand, it is true that we often blame or praise people for their intentions rather than for what actually happens. For example, if someone tries to commit murder, but fails (perhaps he is a lousy shot), we would normally want to blame him. Conversely, a person who kills somebody else purely by an unpreventable accident is not normally considered blameworthy. But at the same time, we *do* judge people by outcomes as well as intentions. There is a distinction in law between murder and attempted murder, with the latter receiving a lighter sentence – with the odd result that we effectively punish people for being more competent. Again, a person who drives a car whilst drunk and kills somebody is likely to be blamed more than one who drives a car whilst drunk and doesn't hit anyone, even if the difference between the two cases is sheer luck. Historians often judge great figures from history on the basis of outcomes rather than intentions. For example, Neville Chamberlain is often judged harshly because he tried to negotiate with Hitler, while Winston Churchill is praised for his uncompromising stance. Yet, of course, both Chamberlain and Churchill wanted to achieve the best outcome possible; they simply disagreed over the best way to do it, and neither could really have known what the best way would be. Historians also judge Anthony Eden to have been a poor prime minister because of his misplaced aggression during the Suez crisis, although Eden claimed that Nasser was as great a threat as Hitler had been. If in fact Nasser had been a new Hitler, perhaps we would think Eden one of the greatest leaders of the twentieth century. And, conversely, if Hitler had been amenable to compromise, we would be praising Chamberlain for his far-sighted commitment to peace and condemning Churchill for his belligerence. It seems that if we are to evaluate such figures on the basis of results – and we certainly do evaluate them in such a way, at least partly – then this has little to do with what they intended.

This suggests that normally we don't see intentions as the be-all and end-all when it comes to evaluating actions. Perhaps this is partly because we tend not to distinguish between the *moral* evaluation of an action and other kinds of evaluation. For example, historians condemn Chamberlain because he failed to recognize the danger that Hitler represented; thus, although his intentions may have been impeccable, he was guilty of poor judgment. In fact, Augustine would regard this as a moral failing too. He takes from Aristotle the idea that we may sometimes be responsible for our own ignorance, and comments:

The soul is charged with guilt, not because by nature it lacks knowledge or is incapable, but because it did not make an effort to know and because it did not work adequately at acquiring the capability of doing well.[1]

This idea was taken even further by Descartes, who in this matter (as well as many others) was greatly influenced by Augustine. He distinguished two major faculties in the mind – the understanding and the will – and argued that the understanding itself never leads us astray. Error occurs when we choose to believe things that the understanding does not clearly show to be true:

> From all this I discover that the power of willing – which I have received from God – is not in itself the source of my errors, for it is extremely sufficient and perfect in its own way. And the power of understanding isn't the source either, for since I conceive no object except by using the faculty that God has given me, everything that I conceive is undoubtedly conceived rightly by me, and it is impossible for me to be deceived in it. So where do my errors come from? They come from this cause alone, that I do not restrain the will – which has a much wider range than the understanding does – within the same limits as the understanding. Instead, I extend it to things I do not understand. And because the will in itself is indifferent to such things, it easily falls into error and sin by choosing the false instead of the true, and evil instead of good.[2]

By this means, Descartes argues that each person is responsible for his or her own mistakes, both intellectual as well as moral. In this view, even scientific error is a sort of sin, because it comes from the misuse of the will. We can't blame God, because he has given us perfectly good tools in the form of our mental faculties; it is up to us to use them correctly.

It may seem rather extreme to make epistemological error a kind of sin or moral failing, but this general approach, of basing moral evaluations upon the intent of the agent, was generally accepted by medieval Christian writers too. Peter Abelard, for example, emphasized the fact that actions are good or bad solely by virtue of the agent's intention, and have nothing to do with the outcome. Aquinas, too, argued that acts are good or bad by virtue of their ends; that is, what the agent hopes to achieve by performing them. In this view, even an apparently innocent action may be very wicked depending on the reason why someone performs it. For example, exercising and becoming physically stronger may be a good thing in itself, but if we do it purely because we want to be able to kick sand in people's faces at the beach, then engaging in a weight-training programme is sinful. Again, if we intend to do something wrong, but are somehow mistaken about right and wrong and accidentally do something right after all, we are still guilty of sin. However, if we intend to do something *right*, but are mistaken about right and wrong and accidentally do something wrong, then we may well be sinning as well – because, like Augustine, Aquinas thinks that ignorance is often culpable. So on Aquinas' terms, it looks as if one is constantly in danger of sinning. In fact, Aquinas holds that every action that we deliberate about – every action which we do with some particular purpose – will be either good or evil, because deliberate intentions are always one or the other. Only non-rational actions, such as idly stroking one's beard, are neither good nor evil.

This emphasis on the will as the faculty by which people make their choices, and on the role of intention in morality, has historically been one of the most important elements in Christian discussions of ethics. But Christians have disagreed over what sort of intention makes actions good or bad. What have some of their views been?

Good for Good's Sake

One quite plausible view aims to take seriously a common-sense view about the sorts of intention one should cultivate. The first-century BC statesman and writer Cicero described the way in which people deliberate about how to behave in terms that seem very familiar even now:

> First, people question whether the contemplated act is morally right or morally wrong; and in such deliberation their minds are often led to widely divergent conclusions. And then they examine and consider the question whether the action contemplated is or is not conducive to comfort and happiness in life, to the command of means and wealth, to influence, and to power, by which they may be able to help themselves and their friends; this whole matter turns upon a question of expediency. The third type of question arises when that which seems to be expedient seems to conflict with that which is morally right; for when expediency seems to be pulling one way, while moral right seems to be calling back in the opposite direction, the result is that the mind is distracted in its inquiry and brings to it the irresolution that is born of deliberation.[3]

In this view, one of the questions that people ask themselves when considering what to do is simply 'Is this the right thing to do?' Some have suggested that this is itself a criterion of rightness. That is, an action is right when it is undertaken with the right intention, and the right intention simply is the desire to do what is right.

The philosopher most strongly associated with this viewpoint is Immanuel Kant. Like the other Christian moralists mentioned above, Kant is clear that rightness or wrongness comes about from intention:

> A good will is good not because of what it performs or effects, not by its aptness for the attainment of some proposed end, but simply by virtue of the volition, that is, it is good in itself, and considered by itself is to be esteemed much higher than all that can be brought about by it in favour of any inclination, nay, even of the sum total of all inclinations. Even if it should happen that, owing to special disfavour of fortune, or the niggardly provision of a stepmotherly nature, this will should wholly lack power to accomplish its purpose, if with its greatest efforts it should yet achieve nothing, and there should remain only the good will (not, to be sure, a mere wish, but the summoning of all means in our power), then, like a jewel, it would still shine by its own light, as a thing which has its own value in itself.[4]

And what is it that makes the will good? Kant notes that the Bible commands us to love our enemies – that is, to behave in a morally upright way even when we would naturally want to do the opposite. But love isn't the sort of thing that one can be commanded to do; we cannot choose to love or not to love. Rather, we are commanded to behave in a certain way. Kant concludes that the requisite attitude is a sense of *duty*. He comments that, often, we perform actions that are our duty, but not *because* they are our duty. For example, we have a duty to take care of ourselves, but most people do this out of instinct, not from a sense of duty; self-preservation is therefore rarely a moral act (although of course it is not an immoral act, since it is in accordance with duty). Again, we have a duty to be kind and generous to other people. But Kant imagines a philanthropist who behaves in this way simply because he enjoys it. Such a person is not behaving morally, because he does not act out of a sense of duty. He goes on:

> Further still; if nature has put little sympathy in the heart of this or that man; if he, supposed to be an upright man, is by temperament cold and indifferent to the sufferings of others... would he not still find in himself a source from whence to give himself a far higher worth than that of a good-natured temperament could be? Unquestionably. It is just in this that the moral worth of the character is brought out which is incomparably the highest of all, namely, that he is beneficent, not from inclination, but from duty.[5]

There is something instinctively appealing about this conception of morality, one captured by the character of six-year-old Calvin in Bill Watterson's comic strip *Calvin and Hobbes*. Calvin believes that Santa Claus distributes presents at Christmas on the basis of the morality of people's behaviour, and in one strip he comments that, having an intrinsically evil nature himself, he should get special preference:

> I wish Santa would publish the guidelines he uses for determining a kid's goodness. For example, how much does he weigh motives? Does he consider the kid's natural predisposition? I mean, if some sickeningly wholesome nerd *likes* being good, it's *easy* for him to meet the standards! There's no challenge! Heck, anyone can be good if he *wants* to be! The true test of one's mettle is being good when one has an innate inclination towards evil. I think one good act by *me*, even if it's just to get presents, should count as *five* good acts by some sweet-tempered kid motivated by the pureness of his heart, don't you?[6]

Of course, Kant would say that if Calvin's behaviour is to count as genuinely good, it would have to be done out of a desire simply to be good, rather than just to get presents, but he would agree that acting in a good way just because we like to do so is morally worthless. And we do normally think that the notion of moral *effort* is important. Imagine that a kleptomaniac, who has always stolen things, sees that someone has dropped their wallet in the street. By great effort, he suppresses his desire to steal and instead runs after the person to hand back the wallet. Surely this is a morally significant action, in a way that it would not be for someone who has no inclination to steal and who would instinctively return the wallet anyway. But, on the other hand, we could also ask which person we would rather be. Is it better to be a recovering kleptomaniac or someone with no inclination to steal in the first place? Which person would a parent want their child to grow into? Would we rather be friends with Kant's jolly philanthropist, or with his cold-hearted man who nevertheless behaves generously out of a sense of duty?

Considerations like this show the difference between ethical systems that focus on what makes acts right (such as Kant's) and those that focus on what sort of person it is most desirable to be. We shall look at Christian answers to the latter question in the next chapter; for now, it is interesting to note that there can be tensions between the answers to the two questions.

Despite Kant's appeal to the New Testament injunction to love others, it may seem that his theory runs quite counter to that injunction. If we act solely out of a sense of duty, are we loving anyone at all? Many Christians have therefore argued for a quite different notion of what sorts of intentions make actions morally significant.

A Copernican Revolution

The sixteenth-century astronomer Nicholas Copernicus was responsible for one of history's greatest shifts in scientific thinking. He was the first modern thinker to suggest that the earth, and the other planets, revolve around the sun, rather than having everything revolve around the earth, as most people had previously thought. This view, known as heliocentrism, had been suggested before by the ancient philosopher Aristarchus of Samos and also by the occasional late medieval writer, and Copernicus was probably influenced by Indian and Muslim writers who had discussed the idea. Moreover, few people in Copernicus' day were persuaded by his ideas; it would be another century before good evidence for it was made available, and another century after that before the question was generally regarded as settled. Nevertheless, Copernicus was the pivotal figure in the emergence of heliocentrism, to such a degree that we often speak of 'the Copernican revolution'.

Christianity fostered something of a Copernican revolution in ethics. In antiquity, ethical theories generally revolved around the self. That is, ancient theorists typically began by considering the nature of human happiness, and how to achieve it. We will look at some of their theories in the next chapter, together with Christian responses to them, but for now it's worth simply noting that to most ancient moralists, ethics was, in a sense, the science of how to be happy. It was, effectively, the study of what is expedient, and not so much the study of what actions are right and wrong (irrespective of their effect on ourselves). Where ancient philosophers do talk of right and wrong actions outside the context of the inculcation of virtue or vice, it is generally in the context of society and its laws. Plato had written that the purpose of laws is to make life as happy as possible for everyone. Certain actions are permitted by the state, because they tend to the general happiness, and others are forbidden because they tend towards general misery. Those who perform the latter can expect to be punished, and this is the prime motivation for not doing them. Thus, obedience to public morality generally comes from a wish to preserve one's own happiness. This applies even where there is no threat of punishment. For example, Cicero noted that people sometimes confess to their crimes out of a guilty conscience, even when there is no fear of discovery. But in such cases, they are still acting as they do in order to make themselves happier, because they would rather face the consequences of their act than endure their own sense of guilt. Cicero does later comment that the first principle of justice is not to harm others: we are necessarily part of a wider society, and our duty is to that society, rather than to ourselves. Nevertheless, the usual idea seems to have been that even apparently altruistic acts, or moral acts, are typically performed out of selfish reasons. We find this idea occurring in parts of the New Testament, too. Paul wrote to the Romans:

For rulers are not a terror to good conduct, but to bad. Do you wish to have no fear of the authority? Then do what is good, and you will receive its approval; for it is God's servant for your good. But if you

do what is wrong, you should be afraid, for the authority does not
bear the sword in vain! It is the servant of God to execute wrath on
the wrongdoer.
Romans 13:3–4

The idea is basically the same as Plato's: we should obey the laws
because we will face dire consequences if we don't. Paul simply makes
the consequences even worse, since in his view the secular authorities
are empowered by God, and their punishments are backed up by
God's power. Conversely, we find the New Testament suggesting that
we should do what is right because we will be rewarded for it. It is
perhaps something of a surprise to find that this notion comes across
repeatedly in the Sermon on the Mount – surprisingly, since, as we
have already seen, this sermon is often associated with the idea that
motives matter just as much as actions. But Jesus is here represented
as recommending his moral precepts to his listeners by appealing to
what are at heart their selfish instincts. In Matthew 5:46, Jesus tells his
followers that if they love only their friends, they won't be rewarded
for it, since everyone does that. The implication is that the motive for
going beyond usual morality and loving even our enemies is that God
will reward us for doing so. Matthew 6:4–6 contrasts the earthly
rewards enjoyed by the ostentatiously charitable with the heavenly
rewards that await those who are charitable in private. The readers of
passages like these are certainly not told to *behave* selfishly – on the
contrary, it is here that we find the famous 'golden rule' of doing to
others as we would have them do to us – but the motive which is
recommended for behaving in such a way seems to be the
consequences for *oneself* of these actions.

This general view was popular with many early Christians. When
the Church Fathers talk about morality – and, specifically, reasons
why people should be moral – it is typically within the framework
of future punishments and rewards. Consider, for example, these
comments by Justin Martyr, addressed to the emperor:

And we are your helpers and allies in promoting peace, more than
any other people are. For we have this belief that it is impossible
for the wicked, the covetous, the conspirator, and for the virtuous
alike, to escape God's attention. And every person goes to eternal

> punishment or salvation according to the worth of his actions. For
> if everybody knew this, no one would choose wickedness even a
> tiny bit, knowing that he would go to the eternal punishment of fire.
> Everyone would restrain themselves as much as possible, and
> decorate themselves with virtue, in order to get the good gifts of
> God and avoid the punishments.[7]

We could call this view a sort of Christian egoism. In ethical
philosophy, egoism can mean one of two things. First, it can mean
the claim that, as a matter of fact, everyone acts out of ultimately
selfish reasons. Even when people help others, it is really just to
assuage their own consciences. Secondly, it can mean the claim that
everyone *should* behave in this way. The first is 'descriptive ethics',
meaning that it seeks only to describe how people actually behave;
the second is 'normative ethics', meaning that it seeks to
recommend a particular way of life to us. An example of a normative
egoist theory would be that of Epicurus, who thought that everyone
should practise enlightened self-interest: the pursuit of pleasure,
rationally done, would lead to the happy life for all. And an example
of a descriptive egoist theory might be that of Thomas Hobbes, the
seventeenth-century English philosopher who believed that all
human beings are basically selfish and hostile to each other, and that
they come together in society and make laws only because each
person thinks it is in his or her own interest to do so.

Yet, of course, Christianity has also featured a strongly anti-
egoist tradition too. Augustine had little time for the sort of
argument employed by Justin Martyr:

> Anyone who thinks he has achieved a victory over sin thinks it in
> vain, if, through nothing but fear of punishment, he avoids doing sin.
> For even though he does not perform the outward action which the
> evil desire prompts him to do, the evil desire itself within him is an
> unconquered enemy. And who will God find innocent who is willing
> to do the forbidden sin if you just remove the fearful punishment?
> And so, even in his volition, anyone who wants to do what is unlawful
> but refrains from doing it because it can't be done safely, is guilty of
> sin. For as far as he is concerned, he would prefer it if there were no
> justice forbidding and punishing sins... So anyone who avoids sin

only because of fear of punishment is an enemy to justice, but he will become the friend of justice if, through love of it, he does not sin, for then he will really be afraid to sin. For the person who only fears the flames of hell is afraid not of sinning but of being burned. But the person who hates sin as much as he hates hell is afraid to sin. This is the 'fear of the Lord', which 'is pure, enduring for ever'. For the fear of punishment has torment, and is not in love; and love, when it is perfect, casts it out.[8]

It is in the Johannine literature that we find the importance of non-self-regarding love expressed most strongly. In John's Gospel, Jesus is represented as teaching his disciples to love and serve each other *without* the context of looking to their own future fate:

[Jesus] got up from the table, took off his outer robe, and tied a towel around himself. Then he poured water into a basin and began to wash the disciples' feet and to wipe them with the towel that was tied around him... After he had washed their feet, had put on his robe, and had returned to the table, he said to them, 'Do you know what I have done for you? You call me Teacher and Lord – and you are right, for that is what I am. So if I, your Lord and Teacher, have washed your feet, you also ought to wash one another's feet. For I have set you an example, that you also should do as I have done to you.'
John 13:4–15

After this, Jesus tells his disciples:

I give you a new commandment, that you love one another. Just as I have loved you, you also should love one another. By this everyone will know that you are my disciples, if you have love for one another.
John 13:34–35

The letter known as 1 John (apparently written by someone familiar with John's Gospel and writing from the tradition, although not the same author) stresses this idea repeatedly. It is here, in particular, that we find love emphasized as the basis of Christian morality. The point has often been made that the word for 'love' used here, *agape*, means selfless, giving love, in contrast with *eros*, which means yearning love or desire. Thus we find the author telling his readers:

> Whoever loves a brother or sister lives in the light, and in such a
> person there is no cause for stumbling. But whoever hates another
> believer is in the darkness, walks in the darkness, and does not know
> the way to go, because the darkness has brought on blindness.
> **1 John 2:10–11**

Indeed, the author of 1 John makes self-forgetting love the basis of
his whole theology:

> Beloved, let us love one another, because love is from God;
> everyone who loves is born of God and knows God. Whoever does
> not love does not know God, for God is love. God's love was
> revealed among us in this way: God sent his only Son into the world
> so that we might live through him. In this is love, not that we loved
> God but that he loved us and sent his Son to be the atoning
> sacrifice for our sins. Beloved, since God loved us so much, we
> also ought to love one another. No one has ever seen God; if we
> love one another, God lives in us, and his love is perfected in us.
> **1 John 4:7–12**

Augustine made some powerful observations on the need for this
principle. He comments, for example, on how people tend to value
objects – and other people – primarily on the basis of how useful
they are to themselves. A human being is more intrinsically valuable
than a horse, but people will pay more for a horse than they will for
a slave. In his *On Christian Doctrine*, Augustine insists that one
should love other people for their own sake, respecting their
intrinsic dignity, and not simply for the sake of what one can get out
of them. This is, perhaps, a criticism of Aristotle, who believed that
people are typically friends with people from whom they derive
some benefit or pleasure. But it is also an anticipation of Kant's
principle that it is intrinsically wrong to treat people as means to an
end; people should be treated as ends in themselves, not simply as
instruments to be used to get what we ourselves want.

The most striking expressions of application of this principle to
philosophical ethics occurred in early modern times. Egoism, at this

time, was quite a fashionable position. One of the most stinging attacks on it was launched by Joseph Butler, the Anglican bishop of Durham and a leading philosopher of religion, in his sermon *Upon the Love of Our Neighbour*. In that sermon, Butler argued that self-love – even the enlightened kind recommended by Epicurus – was not the way to be happy. Indeed, living like that might actually prevent us being happy, just as over-indulging a child will spoil it. He commented:

> The short of the matter is no more than this. Happiness consists in the gratification of certain affections, appetites, passions, with objects which are by nature adapted to them. Self-love may indeed set us on work to gratify these; but happiness or enjoyment has no immediate connection with self-love, but arises from such gratification alone. Love of our neighbour is one of those affections.[9]

In other words, there are many things that make us happy, but among these is behaving in a loving way to other people. It is doing this that makes us happy, but this is not the same thing as doing it *because* it makes us happy. Indeed, the latter may actually be inconsistent with the former. Contrary to what Hobbes thought, true benevolence, without thought for self, is as much part of human nature as selfishness is.

Focus on God

There is another, perhaps even more authentically Christian response to the question 'What kind of intention makes an act good?', and that is that an act is good when it is done with God in mind. This, again, is something we find in the New Testament. Jesus frequently urges his listeners to focus on God alone, and allow other matters to take care of themselves. In Matthew 6:25–34, he tells his disciples not to worry about everyday problems such as where to find food, since God can take care of it. His followers are instead to 'seek first the kingdom of God'. Elsewhere, Jesus is often represented as answering a moral or political question in a theological way. For example, in Luke 20:21–25, Jesus is asked whether it is lawful to pay taxes to Caesar; he answers that one should give to Caesar what is Caesar's, and to God what is God's.

In Matthew 19:16–17, Jesus responds to a question about how to be good with the comment, 'Why do you ask me about what is good? There is only one who is good.' In one important passage, Jesus replicates the teaching of many Pharisees of his day, that the whole Jewish Law revolves around love of God and of other people:

One of the scribes came near and heard them disputing with one another, and seeing that he answered them well, he asked him, 'Which commandment is the first of all?' Jesus answered, 'The first is, "Hear, O Israel: the Lord our God, the Lord is one; you shall love the Lord your God with all your heart, and with all your soul, and with all your mind, and with all your strength." The second is this: "You shall love your neighbour as yourself." There is no other commandment greater than these.' Then the scribe said to him, 'You are right, Teacher; you have truly said that "he is one, and besides him there is no other"; and "to love one's neighbour as oneself", – this is much more important than all whole burnt-offerings and sacrifices.' When Jesus saw that he answered wisely, he said to him, 'You are not far from the kingdom of God.'
Mark 12:28–34

Is it not contradictory to say, on the one hand, that actions should be performed for the sake of other people, without using them as means to an end, and on the other, that actions should be performed for *God's* sake? Later theologians have argued that it is not. Augustine, once again, provides the most detailed discussion. He believed that, although we are commanded to love others just as we love ourselves, the real object of our love should be God. This is an ethical precept as well as a merely theological one, because Augustine suggests that loving the correct things is actually the definition of virtue. The universe is ordered hierarchically, and some beings are intrinsically more worthy of love than others; for example, human beings are more worthy of love than animals, and angels more worthy of love than human beings, although this does depend on their behaviour. A good human being is more deserving of love than a wicked angel. But at the top of the pile is God himself, who is worthy of love above all. Since he is most deserving of love, it cannot be wrong to love him; on the contrary, to do so is the basis of all virtue:

> But if the Creator is truly loved – that is, if he is loved himself and not
> something else in his place, he cannot be loved in an evil way. For
> love itself is to be loved in an orderly way, because we do well to love
> whatever makes us live well and in a virtuous way when we love it.
> So it seems to me that it is a brief but true definition of virtue to say
> that it is the order of love. And because of this, in the Song of Songs,
> the bride of Christ, the city of God, sings, 'Order love within me.'[10]

So to love God truly is actually the same thing as to love other people for their own sakes, because both stem from a correct perception of the natural order of things. Someone who understands reality – and who understands the place of both God and human beings within reality – will love each as they deserve.

Augustine works this principle into his distinction between the two 'cities' – the heavenly city and the earthly city – into which he believes humanity can be divided. These two cities are the subject of the second half of his masterpiece, *City of God*, and they are characterized by what their inhabitants love:

> So two cities have been formed by two loves – the earthly one by
> the love of self, to the extent of holding God in contempt, and the
> heavenly by the love of God, to the extent of holding the self in
> contempt. The former, in a word, glories in itself, and the latter in
> the Lord. For the one looks for glory from men, but the greatest
> glory of the other is God, the witness of conscience. The one lifts
> up its head in its own glory, but the other says to its God, 'You are
> my glory, and you lift up my head.' In the one, the rulers and nations
> that it conquers are ruled by the love of ruling, but in the other, the
> rulers and subjects serve each other in love – the latter obeying,
> the former thinking of everyone.[11]

As this suggests, Augustine thinks that the root of all sin and evil is idolatry. It is the failure of the will of created beings to recognize God for what he is and give him the love and worship that he deserves. This is the fundamentally evil intent that characterizes wrongful acts, just as the correct worship of God is the fundamentally good intent that characterizes right acts.

Other Christian writers have developed the same idea. John Calvin wrote:

> The Christian ought, indeed, to be so trained and disposed as to consider, that during his whole life he has to do with God. For this reason, as he will bring all things to the disposal and estimate of God, so he will religiously direct his whole mind to him. For he who has learned to look to God in everything he does, is at the same time diverted from all vain thoughts. This is that self-denial which Christ so strongly enforces on his disciples from the very outset, which, as soon as it takes hold of the mind, leaves no place either, first, for pride, show, and ostentation; or, secondly, for avarice, lust, luxury, effeminacy, or other vices which are engendered by self-love. On the contrary, wherever it reigns not, the foulest vices are indulged in without shame; or, if there is some appearance of virtue, it is vitiated by a depraved longing for applause.[12]

This emphasis on focusing on God thus became an important element of the Reformed tradition, which took its inspiration from Calvin. One of the most sustained defences of this approach within that tradition was made by the eighteenth-century American theologian Jonathan Edwards in his short but remarkable book *The Nature of True Virtue*. Edwards' theory revolves around a distinction between two kinds of virtue – 'true' and 'natural'. He explains that 'true virtue' consists of a heartfelt love for 'being' itself. It is general in its scope: one does not love a certain thing because it exemplifies some lovable characteristic, but because it is simply *a* thing. So a virtuous person will have a benevolent attitude towards all beings as instantiations of 'being' itself, although Edwards qualifies this by saying that in fact benevolence is exercised only towards intelligent beings, since inanimate things 'are not properly capable objects of benevolence'.[13] As he puts it:

> True virtue most essentially consists in *benevolence to being in general*. Or perhaps, to speak more accurately, it is that consent, propensity and union of heart to being in general, which is immediately exercised in a general good will.[14]

On the basis of this definition, Edwards devotes the second chapter of his book to showing that true virtue must be directed primarily towards God. God has 'being' to a greater degree than anything else; indeed, created things exist only 'in God'. Moreover, God himself has perfect virtue and benevolence, which makes him the supreme object of creaturely virtue as its secondary object as well as its first. So Edwards aims to demonstrate rationally the truth of Augustine's claim that virtue involves, above all, love for God.

> Therefore he that has true virtue, consisting in benevolence to being in general, and in benevolence to virtuous being, must necessarily have a supreme love to God, both of benevolence and complacence. And all true virtue must radically and essentially, and as it were summarily consist in this. Because God is not only infinitely greater and more excellent than all other being, but he is the head of the universal system of existence; the foundation and fountain of all being and all beauty; from whom all is perfectly derived, and on whom all is most absolutely and perfectly dependent; of whom, and through whom, and to whom is all being and all perfection; and whose being and beauty are, as it were, the sum and comprehension of all existence and excellence: much more than the sun is the fountain and summary comprehension of all the light and brightness of the day.[15]

Given all this, we can contrast 'true virtue' with 'natural virtue', which Edwards characterizes as 'secondary and inferior'. The prime difference between primary and secondary virtue, in Edwards' eyes, is one of scope. The former looks to the general, the latter to the particular. And that means that it is not *true* virtue at all. It considers only a part of the whole system, which means that it involves an inevitably inaccurate judgment of reality. This is especially so given that secondary virtue typically overlooks the most important part of the whole system, God himself. This means, in fact, that secondary virtue is not simply distinct from true virtue but is essentially opposed to it:

> These private affections, if they do not arise from general benevolence, and they are not connected with it in their first

existence, have no tendency to produce it. This appears from what
has been observed: for being not dependent on it, their detached
and unsubordinate operation rather implies opposition to being in
general, than general benevolence; as every one sees and owns
with respect to self-love.[16]

In fact, Edwards characterizes it as not simply limited in scope but
revolving around the self. Secondary virtue comes down, ultimately,
to self-interest. Yet Edwards drops something of a bombshell: most
of the character traits that we typically praise as 'virtues', he
suggests, are actually secondary virtues and therefore not true
virtues at all. Most apparently good behaviour that we see in society
really comes from some kind of self-interest and does not stem
from a genuine love for God. He notes, insightfully, that the less
obviously these 'virtues' are based upon self-interest, the more
inclined people are to praise them:

Hence, among the Romans, love to their country was the highest
virtue; though this affection of theirs so much extolled, was
employed as it were for the destruction of the rest of mankind. The
larger the number is, to which that private affection extends, the
more apt men are, though the narrowness of their sight, to mistake
it for true virtue; because then the private system appears to have
more of the image of the universal.[17]

And there's another bombshell in Edwards' conception of the
conscience. Many Christian philosophers of his period regarded the
conscience as a faculty of the mind, put there by God to tell people
right from wrong. On this view, the conscience is almost like one of
the physical senses, except that instead of 'seeing' physical objects it
'sees' moral truths. But Edwards suggests that the conscience 'sees'
only *secondary* virtue. One of the clear signs of this, in Edwards'
view, is that conscience makes no reference to God. It is simply a
sort of psychological reaction to certain actions, a subconscious
attempt to dispel cognitive dissonance caused by inconsistency in
one's attitudes towards others and oneself. We feel bad when we
harm others simply because we would not like others to harm us,
and the inconsistency in our behaviour is unpleasant. So the

promptings of conscience really boil down to selfishness. As Edwards comments, 'All sin has its source from selfishness, or from self-love not subordinate to a regard to being in general.'[18]

Yet this is only half the story, for Edwards also has many positive things to say about natural virtue. He tells us that 'self-love is far from being useless in the world, yea, it is exceeding necessary to society'.[19] Moreover, he is concerned not to disparage the conscience, which he believes is implanted by God and operates according to laws God chose. This is because Edwards thinks that, owing to the brilliant divine design, the objects of natural virtue and true virtue coincide, despite their fundamentally different natures. He stresses this point repeatedly:

> Thus natural conscience, if the understanding be properly enlightened, and stupefying prejudices are removed, concurs with the law of God, is of equal extent with it, and joins its voice with it in every article.[20]

Once again, this is not because natural conscience has anything to do with true virtue. It is because God has established the natural laws that make conscience work in this way. Thus, if we follow the promptings of conscience, we will do what is morally right. But that is still not the same thing as being a good person. Why? The answer, for Edwards, is primarily theological. Those who follow only natural virtue are motivated only by self-interest, although it may be of a relatively enlightened variety – and, as we have seen, he brands self-interest the root of sin. Such an outlook fails to take the most important element of reality – God himself – into account. There is a fundamental paradox here: God has chosen to use self-interest to drive conscience, which in its perfect operation agrees with true virtue and is essential to the good order of society. Edwards is clearly aware of the paradoxical nature of this account:

> Natural conscience tends to restrain sin in general. But this cannot prove these principles themselves to be of the nature of true virtue. For so is this present state ordered by a merciful God, that even self-love often restrains from acts of true wickedness; and not only so, but puts men upon seeking true virtue; yet is not itself true virtue, but is the source of all the wickedness that is in the world.[21]

Following the Rules

It seems that most Christians have agreed that a morally significant act is one that is performed with the right intent. But as our discussion of Jonathan Edwards suggests, a morally significant act may not be the same thing as a *right* act. Edwards thought that it was possible to do what is right without being a good person, because one can do a right act with the wrong intent. If that is so, then we need a separate account of what makes an act right or wrong, as distinct from what makes a person good or bad.

Most Christians have addressed this issue by appealing to rules. The most important theologian to take this approach is Thomas Aquinas, with his theory of the natural and divine laws. Aquinas defines a law as 'an ordinance of reason for the common good, made by him who has care of the community, and promulgated'.[22] Aquinas distinguishes between three kinds of law. Most important is the eternal law, which consists of the moral rules laid down by God himself from all eternity. Some (though not all) of the eternal law can be known by reason, and this is the second kind of law, the natural law. Finally, human beings apply what they know of natural law to their own particular situations, and this is called human law. So, for example, it is part of the eternal law that one must not murder. This is something that everybody knows, even without the need for God to tell them; thus it is part of the natural law too. And human legislators have drawn up various rules to clarify what counts as murder and what doesn't; this is the human law.

The important element, of course, is that it all comes ultimately from God. Aquinas comments:

> Now God, by his wisdom, is the creator of all things, and he is to all
> things what a craftsman is to the things his art has made...
> Moreover, he governs all the actions and movements that are to be
> found in each single created thing... So just as divine wisdom,
> inasmuch as everything is created by it, has the character of art,
> prototype, or idea, so too divine wisdom, inasmuch as it moves all
> things to their proper ends, has the character of law. So the eternal
> law is nothing else than the divine wisdom, directing all actions and
> movements.[23]

As we will see in the next chapter, Aquinas thinks of these rules as issued for our benefit. That is, following the eternal law is the route to a happy life. But this conception of morality does have problems. One is a purely practical problem. What happens when we don't know what the law actually states? Aquinas seems fairly sanguine about our knowledge of morality: much of the eternal law is reflected in the natural law, which everyone knows. Although he accepts that some people disagree about elements of the natural law, he thinks that these are only rare cases, and they are disagreements about details rather than general principles. Even that seems rather an optimistic view, given the many disagreements that there have been – and still are – over ethics. And even if we accept it, it doesn't help much when one is actually in a situation where one has to act but lacks any clear guidance from the law.

Rigorists and Laxity

This problem was the basis of a long-running and rather bitter controversy between the sixteenth and nineteenth centuries, known as the 'probabilism controversy'. A number of sixteenth-century commentators on Aquinas had suggested that, where we don't know what the moral law prescribes, we can at least make a fairly good guess. In particular, we have the writings of earlier theologians and Christian philosophers to help us. Admittedly, they sometimes disagree with each other, which means we are sometimes faced with a number of possible answers to an ethical dilemma; but we need only follow the one that seems most likely to be true. However, a Spanish theologian named Bartholomew de Medina rejected this idea. He argued instead that it is permissible to accept any of the answers which earlier authorities have suggested, not simply the most probable one. He pointed out that the stricter point of view, requiring us always to do what is most probably right, 'tortures frightened minds, for [if it were true] one always ought to inquire into what the more probable opinion is – something which frightened men would never do'.[24]

The storm that this fairly simple idea unleashed was remarkable in its ferocity and duration. Many Jesuits liked Bartholomew's position and defended their own versions of it. But many Dominicans were opposed (although Bartholomew himself had been a Dominican).

There was, at this time, considerable rivalry between these two Catholic orders on a number of matters, including the debate over grace and free will that we saw in chapter 6, which cannot have made for a peaceful atmosphere. Still, those Jesuits who agreed with Bartholomew (dubbed 'probabilists', since they thought it permissible to perform any action considered probably the right one, even if it was not the *most* probably right one) argued that their opponents wanted to impose too strict a morality on people. To insist that one must always perform the action which is most probably the right one is to expect too much, especially in practical situations where one may not have the time or ability to establish what is most likely to be the right thing to do. Rather, if one does something that seems likely to be the right thing to do, without bothering about whether it is marginally more likely to be right than the alternative, that is good enough. But their opponents (dubbed 'probabiliorists', from the Latin for 'more probable', since they believed that one should always do the most probably right action) condemned this approach as moral laxity. If we don't have to do what is most probably right, they argued, then we can do pretty much anything we like provided we can come up with some excuse for it. This was the view of most non-Catholics, too. Many Anglicans condemned probabilism repeatedly, and diatribes against the position could still be found in British journals and books well into the nineteenth century.

The probabilism debate had died out by the end of the nineteenth century, but it represents an eternal problem within Christian ethical thinking, which is how rigorist one should be. That is, how high should moral standards be set? Christians first faced this as a serious practical issue in the second and third centuries AD, in the face of persecution from the Roman state. Many church members buckled in the face of persecution and denied their faith. Later, though, once the persecution ended (for at this time, persecutions against Christians tended to be local and relatively brief), many wanted to be allowed back into the church. The other Christians disagreed over whether they should be let back in. The third century, for example, saw a number of arguments of this kind. In AD 251, in the aftermath of a period of persecution, Cyprian, bishop of Carthage, made a speech to a church council in Carthage. In it, he denounced those who wanted to readmit those who had lapsed in their faith during the persecution. He insisted that a long period of penitence must be imposed upon them, and that the apparent mercy of his opponents was really doing harm to the lapsed and to the church alike:

> All these warnings being scorned and condemned, before their sin is cleansed, before they have made confession for their crime, before their conscience has been purged by sacrifice and the hand of the priest, before the justice of an angry and threatening Lord has been appeased, violence is done to his body and blood. And now they sin against their Lord with their hand and mouth more than when they denied their Lord. They think that those who use deceitful words are championing peace. That is not peace, but war. Whoever is separated from the Gospel is not joined to the church. Why do they call an injury a kindness? Why do they call what is unholy holiness? Why do they stop those who ought to be weeping unstoppably and praying sorrowfully to their Lord in repentance, and pretend to receive them to communion? Let no one cheat himself. Let no one deceive himself. Only the Lord can have mercy. He alone can pardon the sins that have been committed against him – him, who bore our sins, who suffered for us, whom God delivered up for our sins. Man cannot be greater than God... [25]

Some of his opponents pointed out that it was a bit rich of Cyprian to go on like this, given that his own response to the persecutions had been not to confess his faith but to run away and hide. And indeed, a year later, Cyprian relaxed his rule somewhat when a terrible plague broke out, and he allowed the lapsed to return to the church even if they had not completed their penances. Many other Christians, who had agreed with Cyprian's earlier views, broke away from the church, declaring it irrevocably tainted by the sin of the lapsed. Finally, in AD 258, a fresh persecution broke out; this time, Cyprian did not run away, and he died as a martyr. Yet this problem would continue to plague the church for centuries. In the fourth century, a similar dispute about how to treat lapsed Christians resulted in a completely separate church being set up – the Donatist Church – which not only refused to have anything to do with those who had denied their faith, but refused to have anything to do with other Christians who accepted those who had denied their faith. In North Africa, this church was more popular than the mainstream Catholic Church; when Augustine preached in his cathedral in Hippo, he was often interrupted by the loud singing coming from the Donatist Church down the road.

In general, Christians have had to combine a sense of the uncompromising nature of the divine justice with an equal sense of the divine mercy. This is, in part, an issue concerning one's view of God: is he more fundamentally righteous, or more fundamentally loving? That issue was a matter of considerable controversy in the seventeenth-century Reformed Church. Some theologians, notably Jacobus Arminius and Moise Amyrault, argued that God's love, and his will to save people, was more fundamental. They were opposed by others, such as Pierre du Moulin, who insisted that God's justice was more fundamental, and his will to save must be understood only against that background. Of course this problem has its parallel in ethics too. The mainstream view has usually been that one must find a middle course. In the second century, the church condemned the views of Carpocrates, a Gnostic Christian who believed that moral laws were the work not of God but of inferior angels, who had seized control of the world from its true creator. The most ethical life is therefore the most dissolute, and one should try to break as many of these laws as possible. Although temporarily popular in some quarters (as one might expect), this approach did not really catch on. Yet the church also came to reject the opposite view, that an extremely rigorous morality is essential to Christianity. This view was associated with Pelagius, who was condemned in the early fifth century. He believed that human beings are capable of living perfect lives, and that therefore it is incumbent on them to do so. In his view, Christians should, in effect, all live as monks. But the church rejected this. A middle way between Carpocrates and Pelagius became the norm: one where there are standards of morality – quite high ones, perhaps, compared to some – but not impossible ones.

Abandoning the Law?

Other Christians – mostly in more modern times – have rejected the idea of moral 'laws' altogether. Karl Barth, one of the most important theologians of the twentieth century, particularly hated

Aquinas' concept of the 'natural law'. Barth believed that any notion that human beings could know things about God apart from revelation was fundamentally un-Christian: God, in his eyes, is one who acts upon us, not one who is passively sought out by us. As we saw in chapter 2, this means that in his view it is not possible to prove God's existence. But it also applies to ethical matters. Barth regarded the attempt to formulate moral laws and maxims (Aquinas' 'human law') as a basically idolatrous practice; it is the attempt to put human principles at the centre of our lives. In fact, the only thing that should be at the centre of our lives is God himself. Barth thus accepts Augustine's emphasis on placing God at the centre, but makes it even more radical: living ethically means doing what God commands *right now*, not trying to learn some kind of dusty record of what God supposedly said a long time ago.

Another alternative to the traditional view, proposed by a number of twentieth-century Christian thinkers, is situation ethics. This rests upon the insight that it is often impossible to determine what the right thing to do is until one is actually in a given situation. Thus, it is really quite pointless to try to formulate general ethical rules, because once we are actually living our lives and trying to do so in an ethical way, those rules may not seem quite so useful. Does this mean we shouldn't have any ethical principles at all? Of course not – for that would just be complete libertarianism. The American theologian and moral philosopher Joseph Fletcher argued that the middle way between these two extremes – legalism and libertarianism – is found in Jesus' law of love. Remember the passage we saw earlier, where Jesus tells an inquirer that the law can be reduced to the injunction to love God and our neighbour. Fletcher suggests that, in practice, this is all we need. If we really take this principle to our hearts, we will live in an ethical way without needing to formulate any more rules and moral laws. After all, Jesus didn't set out any such rules; he simply told people to make sure that what was in their hearts was right. Fletcher suggested that, most of the time, the moral principles that we actually have (and which have been formulated by Christian moralists such as those we have already looked at) do cover most cases. In other words, situation ethics doesn't mean that we shouldn't have any moral laws at all. But, sometimes, we are faced with very difficult problems that the laws don't help us with. At such times, we must simply try to do the best we can, on the basis of the law of love as taught by Jesus. The important thing is that the law of love is flexible and adapts itself to different situations; we can never say 'never'. Some versions of situation ethics have been proposed according to which one should *almost* never break the moral laws that we have. On this conception, making an exception to the law is permitted in proportion to the reason one has for doing so. For example, lying in order to make some money is not acceptable, but lying to save a life might be. The permissibility of breaking a rule rests upon the moral significance of one's reason for doing so. This approach is known as 'proportionalism'.

Situation ethics and proportionalism were extremely influential in the 1960s, with theologians such as Paul Tillich and Reinhold Niebuhr endorsing similar views. Since then, many have criticized them for being too vague. It's all very well to say we have to be loving in all situations, but does that really offer much guidance? Pope John Paul II attacked situation ethics in his 1993 encyclical *Veritatis Splendor*, where he instead endorsed Thomas Aquinas' belief in divinely sanctioned moral laws that should never be broken, no matter how weighty the apparent justification. Many Christians agree with this view and insist that situation ethics and proportionalism alike abandon the notion of absolute right and wrong in favour of something more akin to secular relativism. It is, in effect, a replay of the old debate between the probabilists and the probabiliorists.

As all this suggests, moral theology is a lot like dogmatic theology. It has to be constructed. The Bible is no more a handbook of systematic ethics than it is one of systematic theology. Just as Christians disagree over points of doctrine, including many we have looked at in this book, so too they disagree over points of ethics. Yet, for all that, we can see some perennial concerns. Most Christian moralists have agreed that God should be the focus of morality, and that the primary rule when dealing with others is love. These are the basic themes of the Sermon on the Mount. How the details are worked out, and how these principles are made practical, is the task of moral theology, and it is a task that is unlikely ever to be completed.

Chapter 10

What is the Ultimate Goal of Life?

What is happiness? Do human beings have a purpose? What is the meaning of life? Such questions are truly perennial; they have been asked for perhaps as long as human beings have been able to ask anything, and no doubt they will continue to be asked for just as long again. It's not always clear if such questions even have any meaning, let alone satisfactory answers. To ask what the 'meaning of life' is may be as nonsensical as asking how heavy a concerto is – how can life even be the sort of thing that has a meaning? But these questions have also been asked by Christians, who have attempted to answer them as well. In this chapter we will see what conclusions some of them have reached.

We saw in chapter 5 that one of the key characteristics of religion is a teleological outlook; that is, a sense that things have a purpose. There, the context was the world as a whole. But this also applies to human beings. Our discussion of life after death in chapter 7 made the point that, for Christians, the fate of each individual is bound up with the fate of the universe as a whole. What does this mean for the Christian understanding of the goal of life?

Human Nature

For Christians, discussion of the purpose of humanity has generally begun with the account in Genesis of the creation of humanity.

Then God said, 'Let us make humankind in our own image,
according to our likeness; and let them have dominion over the fish
of the sea, and over the birds of the air, and over the cattle, and
over all the wild animals of the earth, and over every creeping thing
that creeps upon the earth.' So God created humankind in his
image, in the image of God he created them; male and female he
created them.
Genesis 1:26–27

This passage specifies human beings' relation to the world around them and to God, and gives them a fairly exalted status on both scores. Certainly, Christians typically have agreed that human beings are *significant*. That is, human beings are not simply one species of animal among many others; they are particularly important. Some Christians have gone so far as to claim that God created the whole of the rest of the universe for the sake of human beings, a belief that was widespread in the Middle Ages and later repeated by John Calvin. That belief took something of a knock in modern times, of course, first with the general acceptance of the heliocentric model of the solar system (which displaced the earth – and its human inhabitants – from the centre of the universe), and secondly with the realization in the eighteenth and nineteenth centuries that there existed many other solar systems, a fact which marginalized the earth even more. Today, astronomers know that there are some 100,000,000,000 stars in our galaxy alone, and innumerable galaxies as far as telescopes can see. Moreover, the realization that human beings evolved in a process governed by natural laws operating on chance mutations has made it much harder to agree with Calvin that the world was created for the sake of human beings – for human beings could easily not have evolved at all! Yet the remarkable thing is that Christians still insist that human beings are especially significant. Karl Barth, writing in the middle of the twentieth century, commented:

Man is the creature of the boundary between heaven and earth; he
is on earth and under heaven. He is the being that conceives his
environment, who can see, hear, understand and dominate it: 'Thou
hast put all things under his feet.' He is the essence of a free being

in this earthly world. And the same creature stands beneath heaven; and in the face of the *invisibilia*, of what he cannot conceive or dispose of, he does not dominate but is completely dependent... At this inner boundary of creation stands man, as though even as a creature he had to represent this above and below, and thus, as a creature, to signify his place in a relationship which penetrates into the heights and the depths in quite a different way from that of heaven and earth. Man is the place within creation where the creature in its fullness is concentrated, and at the same time stretches beyond itself; the place where God wishes to be praised within creation, and may be praised.[1]

For Barth, human beings are significant not because of where they live (such as at the centre of the universe, as the medievals thought) but because of their abilities. Only human beings can appreciate their earthly environment and also adopt an attitude to God – look down and up at the same time, as it were. That remains true no matter how cosmically insignificant the planet earth may be. And perhaps this view is quite plausible. Importance is a relational quality, not an absolute one: something is important *to* someone else. Few human beings achieve national or international prominence, yet it does not follow that few human beings are important, because most people are important to someone. And that is all the importance that most people need. Similarly, perhaps human beings are just one species among millions, inhabiting a tiny planet in a vast universe – but does that necessarily make them unimportant to God? There is nothing inconsistent about accepting the minuteness of humanity within the universe while still claiming that human beings are important to God. And the Christian faith in the incarnation expresses this: human beings are important because God became one, and died so that they could be saved.

The Image and Likeness

What does it mean to say that human beings are created in the 'image and likeness' of God? We saw in chapter 1 that, in antiquity, some Christians believed that this referred to a physical likeness: in their view, God was a sort of very big human being. John Wyndham mocked this kind of belief in his novel *The Chrysalids*, set in a post-apocalyptic future where mutation is common. The sternly religious society that emerges believes mutation to be a sign of sin, since God created human beings in his own image and specified the precise form that everyone's body should take. In fact, most Christians have not interpreted the passage as crudely as this. For many, the passage refers not to the body but to the soul. Origen, for example, believed that God is, fundamentally, a mind, although a mind far greater than our minds can comprehend. Nevertheless, there is a basic affinity between the divine mind and human minds, and this is why human beings are described as being created in the image of God. Thomas Aquinas disagreed with Origen about the fundamentally intellectual nature of God (in his view, God is intrinsically incomprehensible, so one cannot call God a mind at all), but he agreed that it is in the intellect that one sees the image of God in humanity. And John Calvin argued that human beings have the image of God because they possess rational souls, which other creatures do not – although because human beings are made by God, every aspect of them displays his image to some extent, just as the whole of creation does.

However, others have interpreted the passage in a quite different way. According to Gregory of Nyssa, writing in the fourth century AD, the image of God in human beings lies in their moral qualities:

Just as painters transfer the forms of human beings to their pictures by using certain colours, giving the copy the properly corresponding tints, so that the beauty of the original may be accurately transferred to the likeness, so I want you to understand that our Creator also, painting the portrait to resemble his own beauty, by adding virtues, just like with colours, shows in us his own sovereignty. And the tints, as it were, which portray his true form, are very varied. Not red or white, or the blending of these (whatever we call it), and not a bit of black to paint the eyebrow and the eye, or shades which combine to depict depressions in the figure, and all such arts which the hands of painters contrive – but instead of these, purity, freedom from passion, blessedness, alienation from all evil, and similar attributes which help to form in human beings the likeness of God – it was colours like these that our Creator used to mark our nature.[2]

Gregory makes several interesting points here. First, human beings are similar to God not because of what they look like or what they are made of but because of their abilities. Furthermore, these are all *moral* abilities. Aristotle had said that human beings resemble God by virtue of their rationality, which means that when we use our reason, we are using the part of us that is most divine and becoming more divine ourselves. But Gregory says that we are more like God when we love than when we reason. Moreover, the image and likeness are not 'fixed'. It is not the case that we simply possess the image and likeness and that's it. Rather, it is up to us to realize the image and likeness, to make it real in ourselves. We do that by actually exercising the God-given moral faculties. Clearly, it is no good simply to have the ability to love, as everyone has that, even the most hateful person alive. It is only when we actually do love people that we mimic God.

The Ordered Soul

The ancient Christians generally believed that a happy life could be attained only within a context of order. Chaos, by contrast, was invariably the work of the devil. As we saw in chapter 2, Christians shared the common belief that God's existence could be proved by considering the nature of the universe, and the quality of that universe which proved God's existence best was its orderliness. But this was mirrored in human nature itself. Plato had said that the human soul contains a higher and a lower part. If it is to function properly, the higher part must direct the lower; otherwise there will be disorder and vice. The Christians extended this idea. Not only must the higher part of the soul direct the lower, but it must itself be subordinate to God. Gregory of Nyssa described a sort of psychic hierarchy: at the top is God, who directs and orders the human mind. The mind directs and orders the lower parts of the soul and the body. In this way, goodness and beauty seep down, as it were, from God to the person, and happiness results. The emphasis on hierarchy comes, in part, from Neoplatonism – although the word 'hierarchy' itself was actually coined by the Christian mystic Pseudo-Dionysius (it means 'holy rule'). This general idea would hold sway over Christian anthropology and ethics for the next thousand years. It received the blessing of Augustine.

> In this, then, consists the righteousness of a man, that he submit
> himself to God, his body to his soul, and his vices, even when they
> rebel, to his reason, which either defeats or at least resists them;
> and also that he beg from God grace to do his duty, and the pardon
> of his sins, and that he render to God thanks for all the blessings he
> receives.[3]

This rather mystical approach to ethics would influence the more legalistic approach that developed during the Middle Ages, which we saw in chapter 9. For Aquinas, living in an orderly fashion means submitting to the natural law which God lays down (rather than to God's direct leadership, as Gregory seems to imagine). The important thing here is that they agree that following God is not simply the way to do what is morally right. It is the way to be happy. And this is because God has designed human beings to live in this way; it is their 'function'.

The Function of a Human Being

The idea that a human being can have a function, like a machine, sounds odd. But in fact this basic conviction was at the heart of most ancient ethical theories, which typically sought to identify what that function was. The idea was that the best kind of life for human beings would involve functioning properly. That does not presuppose that there is any kind of 'intended' function for human beings: it is not as if God has 'designed' them for some purpose. But it still makes sense to talk of function, in the sense of the activity that people are suited to.

The most famous theory of this sort was that of Aristotle, which he presented forcefully in his *Nicomachean Ethics*. In that book, Aristotle suggested that happiness is rather like health: it is a matter of correct functioning. The person who fully realizes his or her potential, who lives the kind of life for which human beings are most suited, will be the happiest. Since the ability to reason is what sets human beings apart from other animals, Aristotle argued that a life devoted to reason would therefore represent the pinnacle of human flourishing, and be the happiest. Nevertheless, since not everyone has the opportunity to spend their lives in philosophical contemplation, it is also possible to find happiness through a practical life, lived out in society, for human beings are also intrinsically social animals. There are thus two kinds of happiness: a rather mundane one, for most people, and a better one, for a select few. Much of Aristotle's book is devoted to an analysis of virtue, for virtues are character traits which tend to produce happiness. So being virtuous is rather like being healthy. Just as we should cultivate (say) lower blood pressure, because it will tend to make us fitter and less prone to certain diseases, so too should we cultivate (say) generosity, because it will make us the sort of person who flourishes and is happy.

Aristotle's theory is often called a 'eudaimonistic' theory, from the Greek word for 'happiness'. It is also often categorized as 'virtue ethics', since it is concerned with cultivating a certain kind of character. His theory had an enormous influence on medieval ethical thought. In particular, Thomas Aquinas modified it in the thirteenth century to produce a Christian theory of happiness and the virtues. Just like Aristotle, Aquinas believes there are two kinds of happiness, but he argues that these two kinds of happiness are nurtured by completely different sets of virtues. In his view, there are actually three kinds of virtue. The first are the intellectual virtues, wisdom, science and understanding, which help one to learn the truth. The second are the moral or cardinal virtues, justice, temperance, fortitude and prudence, which help one to live rightly. Fostering these virtues will produce a lower kind of happiness – what one might call a satisfying life on earth. However, there is also the third kind of virtue, the theological virtues – faith, hope and love (or charity) – which help one to reach one's true destiny and happiness. The list of theological virtues comes from 1 Corinthians 13:13, where Paul also comments that love is the greatest of the three – but he does not specify what their roles are or even call them 'virtues' at all.

Aquinas shares with Aristotle the belief that the intellectual and cardinal virtues can be acquired through practice. If someone behaves justly, he or she will eventually become a just person. But the theological virtues are not like this. They can come only directly from God, and, furthermore, they perfect the other kinds of virtues. It is possible, for example, to have wisdom and justice without also having faith and love; but if we do have faith and love, then our wisdom and justice will be of a higher order, and will contribute to a higher kind of happiness.

The theological virtues, of course, are directed towards God: it is God in whom one has faith and hope, and God whom one loves. In other words, Aquinas is suggesting that a truly virtuous life is one that takes account of God. This is precisely the same point that we saw in the last chapter: according to most Christian moralists, God must be the focus of morality. That is partly because God, who lays down the eternal law, is in effect the creator of morality: things are right or wrong because he says so. From a purely pragmatic point of view, too, God is the creator of human beings: he designed them to function in a certain way. It is therefore wise to pay attention to his operating instructions, as it were.

So in Aquinas' view, it is not simply the case that one must focus on God if one is to act morally (as we saw in the last chapter); one must also focus on God if one is to be happy. Here he was taking his cue from Augustine of Hippo. Augustine's *Confessions*, probably the most famous and influential autobiography ever written, testifies to his belief that happiness can be found only in God. It describes his spiritual wanderings before he finally returned to the church and found happiness. In the first chapter, in undoubtedly the most hackneyed quotation from his entire works, Augustine summarizes the relationship between God and humanity:

> You move us to delight in praising you; for you have formed us for yourself, and our hearts are restless until they find rest in you.[4]

C.S. Lewis expressed the same idea in more modern terms:

> God made us: invented us as a man invents an engine. A car is made to run on petrol, and it would not run properly on anything else. Now God designed the human machine to run on Himself. He Himself is the fuel our spirits were designed to burn, or the food our spirits were designed to feed on. There is no other. That is why it is just no good asking God to make us happy in our own way without bothering about religion. God cannot give us a happiness and peace apart from Himself, because it is not there. There is no such thing.[5]

Aquinas agrees with this. In his view, however, real happiness can never be found in this life. The reason is that we can know God only imperfectly in this life. On earth, the best we can hope for is a satisfying life, the life of morality which comes through exercising the cardinal virtues. If God gives us the theological virtues too, we can begin to glimpse the greater kind of happiness, but we cannot know it fully yet.

> Now man's happiness is twofold... One is proportionate to human nature, a happiness, that is, which human beings can obtain by using their natural abilities. The other is a happiness beyond human nature, and which humans can obtain by the power of God alone, by a kind of participation of the Godhead, which is why it is written that by Christ we are made 'partakers of the divine nature'. And because such happiness surpasses the capacity of human nature, human beings' natural abilities which enable them to act well according to their capacity are not enough to direct them to this same happiness. So it is necessary for humans to receive from God some additional abilities, so that they can be directed to supernatural happiness... Such principles are called 'theological virtues': first, because their object is God, inasmuch as they direct us reliably to God; second, because they are infused in us by God alone; third, because these virtues are not made known to us except by divine revelation, contained in Holy Scripture.[6]

For Aquinas, achieving true happiness is the true function of human beings. What, then, is the nature of this happiness?

The Vision of God

In the West, Christians' understanding of the purpose of human beings – and the nature of their happiness – was enormously influenced, like so much else, by Augustine of Hippo. Four centuries earlier, Paul had written:

> We know only in part, and we prophecy only in part; but when the complete comes, the partial will come to an end. When I was a child, I spoke like a child, I thought like a child, I reasoned like a child; when I became an adult, I put an end to childish ways.

For now we see in a mirror, dimly, but then we will see face to face. Now I know only in part; then I will know fully, even as I have been fully known.
1 Corinthians 13:9–12

It was Augustine who elaborated on this to produce Western Christianity's understanding of the 'now, but not yet' idea that we have just seen in Aquinas: the belief that we can have some dim grasp of future happiness now, but no more than that. Augustine argued that the passage from 1 Corinthians referred to the time following the general resurrection of the dead, after Christ had judged all human beings – that is, the time of eternal life.

And so, when I am asked what the saints will do in that spiritual body, I do not say what I see, but I say what I believe, according to what I read in the psalm, 'I believed, therefore have I spoken.' I say, then, that in the body they will see God – but whether they shall see him by means of the body, as now we see the sun, moon, stars, sea, earth, and all that is in it, that is a difficult question.[7]

Augustine believed that, in the future life, people would 'see' God in the same way that they 'see' each other now. Modern philosophers often talk of 'the problem of other minds'; namely, how can we be certain that the people we see around us are really people like us, with minds and thoughts of their own? After all, we can only see their bodies. Augustine points out that although we cannot literally see other people's minds, we know that they have them from the way that they behave. There is a sense in which we can 'see' other people's minds, although we do not do so literally. And this, he suggests, is what the vision of God will be like in the resurrection life. In this life, we can 'see' God in the world around us only faintly, and we need faith to do so; but in the future life, we will 'see' God in the world around us directly.

Aquinas repeated this notion of the 'beatific vision', but he believed it was even more dramatic than Augustine had suggested. Rather than 'seeing' God in the world around them, Aquinas argued that the saints would 'see' God directly – that is, God's essence, the very divinity of God.

Final and perfect happiness can consist of nothing else than the vision of the divine essence. To make this clear, two points must be observed. First, that human beings are not perfectly happy as long as there is still something for them to desire and seek. Second, the perfection of any power is determined by the nature of its object. Now the object of the intellect is 'what a thing is', i.e. the essence of a thing... So the intellect attains perfection, in so far as it knows the essence of a thing... So, for perfect happiness, the intellect needs to reach the very essence of the First Cause. And thus it will have its perfection through union with God as with that object, in which alone human happiness consists.[8]

In the late Middle Ages, there was some controversy over when, precisely, people could expect to enjoy this beatific vision. As we saw in chapter 7, the orthodox Christian belief in the Middle Ages was that, at death, the soul goes to heaven (or hell), where it waits until the general resurrection from the dead. At this point it is reunited with its body and judged. Augustine had spoken of the beatific vision as a reward that comes after this judgment. But what about the souls waiting in heaven right now? Many people in the Middle Ages thought that they might be allowed to enjoy the beatific vision too. In the early fourteenth century, Pope John XXII denied that they could. His successor, Benedict XII, overruled John's views and issued the following decree in 1336:

We define that the souls of all the saints in heaven have seen and do see the divine essence by direct intuition and face to face, in such a way that nothing created intervenes as an object of vision, but the divine essence presents itself to their immediate gaze, unveiled, clearly and openly; moreover, that in this vision they enjoy the divine essence, and that, in virtue of this vision and this enjoyment, they are truly blessed and possess eternal life and eternal rest.[9]

This has been the orthodox Catholic view ever since.

Union with God

The belief of the Eastern Orthodox churches has, historically, been rather different. Where Catholicism has held that the faithful will see God, the Orthodox have insisted that the faithful will be *united* to God. We saw in chapter 7 how immortality, for some Orthodox theologians, is a matter of the human soul becoming so close to God that it is impossible to tell the difference. For many Christians, indeed, this is what salvation is, a notion that can be derived from the New Testament. In 1 Corinthians 15:54, Paul writes that, at the resurrection, the bodies of believers will become incorruptible and immortal. But, according to 1 Timothy 6:16, these qualities belong to God alone; the future life, then, will be one of sharing in God's qualities. 2 Peter 1:4 tells its readers that they will 'become participants in the divine nature'. As the fourth-century theologian Athanasius famously put it, '[God] became man so that man could become God'.[10]

The Christian writer most associated with this idea in its early centuries was Gregory of Nazianzus, who was briefly patriarch of Constantinople until he was deposed in AD 381. Gregory, known as the Theologian for his work in seeking to understand the Trinity, coined the Greek term *theosis* to express his hope for the future of humanity. *Theosis* literally means 'deification', and Gregory believed that this is something that will happen to the whole person, not just the soul. For Gregory, this would happen above all at the end of time, at the final resurrection:

God will be all in all in the time of restitution... when we shall be no longer divided (as we now are by movements and passions) and containing nothing at all of God, or very little, but shall be entirely like.[11]

But this is something that comes only through Christ. Like Athanasius before him, Gregory was convinced that salvation comes through the fact that, in Christ, humanity and divinity meet. And Christians can hope to share in this meeting themselves. Gregory speaks almost as though human nature and divine nature are tangible 'things' that can literally touch. Since the divine nature has 'touched' human nature in Christ, it is now accessible to everyone, meaning that, through Christ, everyone can hope to become divine:

> In the character of the form of a servant, [Christ] comes down to his
> fellow servants – no, to his servants, and he takes on a strange
> form, bearing all of me and mine in himself, so that in himself he
> may bring evil to an end, as fire does wax, or as the sun does the
> mists of earth; and so that I may share in his nature by the
> blending.[12]

Although Gregory of Nazianzus would always be closely associated
with the doctrine of deification, another name frequently invoked
by later theologians was that of Maximus the Confessor. This
seventh-century monk was most famous for his strident opposition
to the official doctrine, endorsed by the Byzantine emperor, that
Christ had one will (a divine one). Maximus believed that this
doctrine denied Christ's true humanity, and for his views, he was
arrested and had his right hand cut off and his tongue torn out.
Later, however, Maximus' views were vindicated at the Third
Council of Constantinople, and he became revered as a confessor
(one step down from a martyr). Why was this issue so important?
Maximus believed that any denial of the true union of God and
humanity in Christ was, in effect, a denial of the possibility that
anyone else might be united to God. Like earlier theologians,
Maximus was convinced that it is through the incarnation that God
touches humanity: through faith, human beings can become united
to Christ, and this means they are united to God.

> In the same way in which the soul and the body are united, God
> should become accessible for participation by the soul and, through
> the soul's intermediary, by the body, in order that the soul might
> receive an unchanging character, and the body, immortality; and
> finally that the whole man should become God, deified by the grace
> of God-become-man, becoming whole man, soul and body, by
> nature, and becoming whole God, soul and body, by grace.[13]

So for Maximus, deification does not mean ceasing to be human. On
the contrary, it means becoming perfectly human. Christ was not just
fully God; he was also fully human. Becoming united to him means
becoming fully human, just as it means becoming God. Moreover,
union with God means being able to realize one's full potential as a

human being. But Maximus does distinguish between being fully human 'by nature' and being fully God 'by grace'. Even union with God does not mean undifferentiated union; one does not literally 'become' God. One participates in what God is, by grace.

Maximus was enormously influential on later Orthodox theologians. One of the most important of these was the fourteenth-century monk Gregory Palamas. Palamas prefers to use the metaphor of light to describe both what the mystical experience is like and how it can involve union with God:

> This… light, seen spiritually by the saints, they know by experience to exist, as they tell us, and to exist not just symbolically, like manifestations produced by fortuitous events; but it is an illumination immaterial and divine, a grace invisibly seen and ignorantly known. *What* it is, they do not pretend to know.[14]

For Palamas, the fact that this divine light can be (and has been) experienced by mystics means that the future goal of union with God is not some pie-in-the-sky hope that has no direct connection to our current lives; on the contrary, it is simply the logical conclusion of what begins in *this* life. He points out that with literal light, we can see it only because of its own presence: light is seen in light. Similarly, with the divine light, we can see it only because we begin to take on its characteristics. This means that the vision of God necessarily involves becoming united to God:

> For it is in light that the light is seen, and that which sees operates in a similar light, since this faculty has no other way in which to work. Having separated itself from all other beings, it becomes itself all light and is assimilated to what it sees, or rather, it is united to it without mingling, being itself light and seeing light through light. If it sees itself, it sees light; if it beholds the object of its vision, that too is light; and if it looks at the means by which it sees, again it is light. For such is the character of the union, that all is one, so that he who sees can distinguish neither the means nor the object nor its nature, but simply has the awareness of being light and of seeing a light distinct from every creature.[15]

So for Palamas, it is not as if the idea of deification were a sort of alternative to the Western ideal of the 'vision of God'. Rather, it is its logical consequence. The ultimate goal for human beings is to see God, but to see God is to become God. Indeed, he goes beyond this to suggest that the doctrine of deification is an essential part of the Christian doctrine of God itself. The reason is that, for a Christian, God is what gives human beings direction and purpose. But that means that, despite his intrinsic incomprehensibility, God must be ultimately accessible. This is the role of Christ, in whom God and humanity are perfectly and genuinely united, and who paves the way, as it were, for other human beings to become united to God. Without this possibility, God would not be 'God' for us; he would have no meaning and relevance to human life:

> Since there are those who participate in God, yet on the other hand the superessential essence of God is absolutely imparticipable, there must be something between the incommunicable essence and those who communicate of it... If you destroy this... you separate us from God, breaking the bond and setting up a great and unbridgeable gulf. We should then have to seek another God... a God who would be somehow accessible, in whom each one sharing in proportion as he might, could be, and live, and become, godly.[16]

How literally should we take this language? Does Palamas think that each Christian is in the process of becoming, quite literally, a God? Some groups within the Orthodox world have seemed to endorse this idea. The Isochrists of the sixth century were one such group. These Christians – whose name means 'like Christ' – believed that, at the final resurrection of the dead, all Christians would become literally equal to Christ. We saw in chapter 7 that Paul had taught that Christ was the 'first fruits' of the resurrection, that is, the first person to be raised by God, and that everyone would be raised in a similar way. The Isochrists simply took this further, suggesting that if everyone was going to experience what Christ did, then everyone would be exactly the same as Christ; he was just the first. But the Isochrists were condemned for this. So too were the *Khlysty*, a mystical group in the eighteenth-century

Russian church. They believed that God was constantly becoming incarnate in a series of messiahs, and that through the practice of ecstatic prayer, any Christian could receive the Holy Spirit and become indistinguishable from Christ.

Palamas, however, stresses that Christians should not look forward to becoming equal to God. Just like Maximus before him, he points out that union with God means taking on the 'glory' of God, but not his nature:

Thus to our human nature he has given the glory of the Godhead, but not the divine nature; for the nature of God is one thing, his glory another, even though they are inseparable from each other.[17]

The Goal of Life?

How plausible are the views we have been considering here? The common theme is that human beings need God to be truly happy. For example, if Gregory of Nyssa's account of the proper relationship between God and the mind is correct, then an autonomous life will be an unhappy one: order, and peace, and general happiness can occur only where one puts one's mind in subjection to God. The obvious problem with this account is that many people do not do this but seem to be perfectly happy anyway. There are two main possible responses to this. The first is to say that perhaps such people – or at least some of them – really *are* subjecting themselves to God, even though they may not realize it. In Aquinas' language, perhaps God can give someone the theological virtues without their being conscious of it or of him at all. This would be to adopt a stance similar to the one I called 'realized inclusivism' in chapter 8.

An alternative answer to the problem of happy atheists is to suggest that such people *think* they are happy, but they are not really. That may sound rather a patronizing judgment, but it is the essence of Thomas Aquinas' distinction between the moral virtues and the theological virtues, and the two kinds of happiness they bring. In Aquinas' eyes, the non-Christian Aristotle could lead a moral and therefore happy life simply by following the virtues he described using reason alone. However, *true* happiness can come only from following the theological virtues, which can be acquired only with divine aid. And this happiness can be experienced in this life, but only imperfectly.

We could ask how plausible Aquinas' understanding is of the nature of both kinds of happiness. Following Aristotle, he dismisses a number of alternative understandings of the 'lower' kind of happiness, such as the claim that happiness is simply a matter of pleasure. This was the view of Epicurus, who was regularly denounced in late antiquity as a terrible libertine who thought that everyone should just try to cram as much physical pleasure into their time as possible. In fact, Epicurus did not believe this; on the contrary, he pointed out that an unrestrained lifestyle will actually produce more pain than pleasure, as anyone who has experienced a 'morning after the night before' will know. He recommended instead that people should pursue simple pleasures, such as wholesome food, natural surroundings and stimulating company; in the long term, this would be the most pleasant lifestyle. This seems quite an attractive definition of the good life, and many modern philosophers have restated versions of it. Is Aquinas right to reject it?

Perhaps more importantly, though, is the notion of the 'vision of God' an adequate account of the goal of humanity? It seems a slightly curious notion, that human beings could be content spending the whole of eternity simply staring at God. Aquinas argues that God is quite sufficient for anyone's happiness; thus, in this future life, people will not need friends, for example. Everyone's attention will be fixed on God alone. The prospect seems really quite inhuman: surely a happy life that is still recognizably human would involve the society of other people, at least. Origen apparently thought that an eternal vision of God could get boring; this, at least, seems to have been his explanation for the fall of the souls of created beings at the beginning of time. They were created to gaze rapturously at God for ever, but some of them became tired of it. Aquinas, of course, shared the belief of Gregory of Nyssa that God is infinite, which means that no matter how long we spend in contemplation of God there are always more things to discover; with every horizon reached, new ones open up. Aquinas might say that if the vision of God sounds uninteresting, that is only because we lack the imaginative or cognitive abilities to understand it. Still, even if this is true, it sounds as if we would have to undergo significant changes even to understand the vision of God, let alone experience it. This ties in with what we saw in chapter 7 about life after death. The traditional Christian understanding of life after death does involve a vision of a life very different from what we would recognize as human in any meaningful sense. Is that an objection to it? That entirely depends on how much we value being human. Perhaps we do not like the idea of Aquinas' vision of God; but God could change us to creatures who would like the idea. But would we like to be changed?

These considerations could also apply to the Orthodox doctrine of divinization. Here we have a more explicit notion of human beings being changed into something quite different. The idea is again hard to understand. What would it be like to be united to God in such a way? Would we remember our earthly lives? If so, how? And if not, would we still be *us* in any meaningful way? Some might think that Augustine's version of the 'vision of God' seems perhaps more plausible, for in his view it is a sort of heavenly society, where the saints actually live together communally and 'see' God indirectly in the world about them. It seems, at least, more easily imaginable, and so both more recognizable and more desirable.

Endnotes

Introduction
1. Tertullian, *The Prescription against Heretics* 7.
2. Thomas Aquinas, *Summa contra Gentiles* 1.2.

Chapter 1
1. Cassian, *Conferences* 10.3.
2. Joseph Smith, *Doctrines and Covenants* 130.22.
3. Tertullian, *Against Praxeas* 7.
4. Origen, *On First Principles* 1.5–6.
5. Clement of Alexandria, *Miscellanies* 5.11.
6. Pseudo-Dionysius, *Mystical Theology* 3.
7. Marcus Minucius Felix, *Octavius* 32.
8. Anselm of Canterbury, *Proslogion* 8.
9. Friedrich Nietzsche, *Twilight of the Idols and the Anti-Christ*, Harmondsworth: Penguin, 1968 (tr. R.J. Hollingdale), section 18.
10. Thomas Altizer, *The Gospel of Christian Atheism*, Philadelphia: Westminster Press, 1966, pp. 68–69.
11. Don Cupitt, *The Sea of Faith*, London: BBC Books, 1984, p. 263.
12. Cupitt, pp. 269–70.

Chapter 2
1. Karl Barth, *Dogmatics in Outline*, London: SCM Press, 1949 (tr. G.T. Thomson), pp. 37–38.
2. Marcus Minucius Felix, *Octavius* 17.
3. Henry More, *A Collection of Several Philosophical Writings of Dr Henry More* (4th edn), London: Downing, 1712, vol. 2, p. 81.
4. Thomas Aquinas, *Summa Theologiae* 1.2.3.
5. Immanuel Kant, *Critique of Practical Reason*, Cambridge: Cambridge University Press, 1997 (tr. Mary Gregor), p. 133.
6. C.S. Lewis, *Mere Christianity*, London: Fontana, 1955, p. 6.
7. Lewis, p. 7.
8. Lewis, p. 25.
9. Francis Hutcheson, 'An inquiry concerning moral good and evil', in *An Inquiry into the Original of Our Ideas of Beauty and Virtue*, London, 1725, section VII.
10. Pat Robertson, speech to The Concerned Women Of America, 27 July 1985. Available at: http://www.patrobertson.com/Statesman/ConcernedCitizens.asp
11. Tertullian, *On the Testimony of the Soul* 1.
12. Tertullian, *On the Testimony of the Soul* 5.
13. Tertullian, *Apology* 17.
14. Descartes, *Meditations* 3.

Chapter 3
1. Voltaire, 'Poem on the Lisbon Disaster', in *Toleration and Other Essays*, New York: G.P. Putnam's Sons, 1912 (tr. Joseph McCabe).
2. Lactantius, *On the Anger of God* 13.
3. Augustine, *Confessions* 7.12.
4. Mary Baker Eddy, 'Christian Theism', in *Miscellaneous Writings (1883–96)*, Boston: Christian Science Publishing Society, p. 12.
5. Origen, *Against Celsus* 6.55.
6. Helena Blavatsky, *The Secret Doctrine*, I.2.11, London: Theosophical Publishing, 1888, vol. 1, p. 13.
7. Gregory of Nyssa, *Concerning Infants Who Have Died Prematurely*.
8. Irenaeus of Lyon, *Against Heresies* 3.20.2.
9. Origen, *Against Celsus* 6.56.
10. Augustine, *Against the Manichaeans* 1.
11. Abu Hamid al-Ghazali, *Golden Means of Dogmatics*.
12. Origen, *Against Celsus* 4.66.
13. Julian of Norwich, *Revelations of Divine Love* 27.
14. Julian of Norwich, *Revelations of Divine Love* 20.

Chapter 4
1. Douglas Adams, *The Hitch Hiker's Guide to the Galaxy*, London: Pan, 1979, p. 50.
2. Thomas Aquinas, *Summa Contra Gentiles* 1.3.
3. Thomas Aquinas, *Summa Theologiae* 1.1.8.
4. John Locke, *An Essay Concerning Human Understanding*, IV.18.2, Harmondsworth: Penguin, 1997 (ed. Roger Woolhouse), p. 608.
5. Locke, IV.18.5, p. 610.
6. Locke, IV.17.24, p. 607.
7. William Clifford, *The Ethics of Belief* (1877), in Michael Petersen *et al.* (eds), *Philosophy of Religion: Selected Readings* (2nd edn), New York and Oxford: Oxford University Press, 2001, p. 84.
8. Clifford, in Peterson *et al.*, p. 85.
9. Locke, IV.18.2, p. 608.
10. Alvin Plantinga, *Warranted Christian Belief*, New York and Oxford: Oxford University Press, 2000, p. 191.
11. Plantinga, p. 264.
12. Thomas Aquinas, *Summa Theologiae* 2.2.1.4.

Chapter 5
1. Clement of Alexandria, *The Instructor* 1.7.
2. Tertullian, *The Prescription against Heretics* 7.
3. Tertullian, *On the Flesh of Christ* 5.
4. Tertullian, *The Prescription against Heretics* 7.
5. Robert Bellarmine, *Letter to Paolo Foscarini* (1615), quoted in Arthur Koestler, *The Sleepwalkers*, Harmondsworth: Penguin, pp. 454–55.
6. Charles Babbage, *Ninth Bridgwater Treatise* (2nd edn), London: Murray, 1838, pp 78–79.
7. John William Draper, *History of the Conflict between Religion and Science*, London: King, 1875.
8. Stephen Jay Gould, 'Two separate domains', in Michael Petersen *et al.* (eds) *Philosophy of Religion: Selected Readings* (2nd edn), New York and Oxford: Oxford University Press, 2001, pp. 500–501.
9. Anthony Freeman, 'Theology and the Church', *Modern Believing*, 1994, vol. 35, no. 4.

Chapter 6

1. Justin Martyr, *Second Apology* 7.
2. John Calvin, *Institutes of the Christian Religion*, II.5.1–2, London: Knox, 1960 (tr. Ford Lewis Battles). Original edition 1559.
3. Augustine, *On Free Will*.
4. Martin Luther, *On the Enslaved Will*, section 91, 1525.
5. Boethius, *The Consolation of Philosophy* 5.
6. Calvin, I.16.4.
7. Origen, *Against Celsus* 4.70.
8. Luis de Molina, *Disputation* 52.29.

Chapter 7

1. Plato, *Phaedo* 106e–107a.
2. Augustine, *City of God* 13.8.
3. Matthew Tyndale, *An Answer to Sir Thomas More's Dialogue*, 1531.
4. Karl Barth, *Dogmatics in Outline*, London: SCM Press, 1949 (tr. G.T. Thompson), p. 154.
5. Origen, *Homilies on Song of Songs* 1.2.
6. Anonymous, *The Cloud of Unknowing* 5.
7. Maximus the Confessor, *Ambiguities*.

Chapter 8

1. Quoted in Robert Marshall, *Storm from the East: From Genghis Khan to Khubilai Khan*, Berkeley: University of California Press, 1993.
2. '"The journey of William of Rubruck" by himself', in Christopher Dawson (ed.), *The Mongol Mission*, London and New York: Sheed and Ward, 1955, p. 195.
3. Augustine, *City of God* 19.27–28.
4. Cyprian of Carthage, *Letter* 61.
5. Ignatius of Antioch, *Letter to the Philadelphians* 3.3.
6. Martin Luther, *That Jesus Christ Was Born a Jew*, 1523.
7. Jerome, *Commentary on Titus* 3.10–11.
8. Francis Xavier, *The Letters and Instructions of Francis Xavier*, St Louis, MO: Institute of Jesuit Sources, 1992 (tr. M. Joseph Costelloe), pp.117–18. Original source 1545.
9. Luca da Caltanisetta, quoted in Bengt Sundkler and Christopher Steed, *A History of the Church in Africa*, Cambridge: Cambridge University Press, 1998.
10. Origen, *Homilies on Joshua* 3.5.
11. Origen, *On First Principles* 2.10.3.
12. Justin Martyr, *First Apology* 46.
13. Karl Rahner, in Michael Petersen *et al.* (eds), *Philosophy of Religion: Selected Readings* (2nd edn), New York and Oxford: Oxford University Press, 2001, p. 554.
14. Rahner, in Petersen *et al.*, p. 555.
15. Second Vatican Council, *Dogmatic Constitution on the Church: Lumen Gentium*, section 16, 21 November 1964.
16. John Hick, in Petersen *et al.*, p. 566.
17. Hick, p. 570.
18. Thomas Hobbes, *Leviathan* 31.33, Harmondsworth: Penguin, 1968 (ed. C.B. Macpherson).

Chapter 9
1. Augustine, *On Free Will* 3.22.64.
2. Descartes, *Meditations* 4.9.
3. Cicero, *On Duties* 1.3.
4. Immanuel Kant, *Fundamental Principles of the Metaphysic of Ethics*, London: Longmans, Green and Co., 1946 (tr. Thomas Kingsmill Abbott), p. 11.
5. Kant, p. 17.
6. Bill Watterson, *Homicidal Psycho Jungle Cat*, London: Warner, 1994, p. 30.
7. Justin Martyr, *First Apology* 12.
8. Justin Martyr, *Letter* 145.4.
9. Joseph Butler, 'Upon the love of our neighbour', in *Fifteen Sermons Preached at the Rolls Chapel*, London: Knapton, 1726, XI, section 16.
10. Augustine, *City of God* 15.22.
11. Augustine, *City of God* 14.28.
12. John Calvin, *Institutes of the Christian Religion* III.8.2, London: Knox, 1960 (tr. Ford Lewis Battles). Original edition 1559.
13. Jonathan Edwards, *The Nature of True Virtue*, Ann Arbor, MI: University of Michigan Press, 1960, p. 5.
14. Edwards, p. 3.
15. Edwards, p. 15
16. Edwards, p. 78.
17. Edwards, p. 88.
18. Edwards, p. 92.
19. Edwards, p. 89.
20. Edwards, p. 68.
21. Edwards, p. 95.
22. Thomas Aquinas, *Summa Theologiae* 1.2.90.4.
23. Thomas Aquinas, *Summa Theologiae* 1.2.93.1.
24. Bartholomew de Medina, *Commentary on the Summa* 1.2.19.6.
25. Cyprian of Carthage, *On the Lapsed* 16–17.

Chapter 10
1. Karl Barth, *Dogmatics in Outline*, London: SCM Press, 1949 (tr. G.T. Thomson), p. 63.
2. Gregory of Nyssa, *On the Making of Man* 5.
3. Augustine, *City of God* 19.27.
4. Augustine, *Confessions* 1.1.
5. C.S. Lewis, *Mere Christianity*, London: Fontana, 1955, p. 50.
6. Thomas Aquinas, *Summa Theologiae* 1.1.62.1.
7. Augustine, *City of God* 22.29.
8. Thomas Aquinas, *Summa Theologiae* 1.2.3.8.
9. *Benedictus Deus* (1336) [Papal decree].
10. Athanasius, *On the Incarnation* 54.
11. Gregory of Nazianzus, *Oration* 30.6.
12. Gregory of Nazianzus, *Oration* 30.6.
13. Maximus the Confessor, *Ambiguities*.
14. Gregory Palamas, *Triads* 2.3.8.
15. Gregory Palamas, *Triads* 2.3.36.
16. Gregory Palamas, *Triads* 3.22.24.
17. Gregory Palamas, *Triads* 2.3.15.

Further Reading on the Subject of Philosophy of Religion

Abraham, W. and Holtzer, W., eds. *The Rationality of Religious Belief,* Oxford: Clarendon, 1987.

Adams, M. and Adams, R., eds. *The Problem of Evil,* Oxford: Oxford University Press, 1990.

Cahn, S. *God, Reason, and Religion,* Belmont, CA: Wadsworth, 2006.

Davis, S. *Logic and the Nature of God,* London: Macmillan, 1983.

Dole, A. and Chignell, A., eds. *God and the Ethics of Belief,* Cambridge: Cambridge University Press, 2005.

Gale, R. *On the Nature and Existence of God,* Cambridge: Cambridge University Press, 1991.

Hester, M., ed. *Faith, Reason and Skepticism,* Philadelphia, PA: Temple University Press, 1992.

Howard-Snyder, D., ed. *The Evidential Argument from Evil,* Bloomington, IN:Indiana University Press, 1996.

Kenny, A. *The God of the Philosophers,* Oxford: Clarendon, 1979.

Mackie, J. *The Miracle of Theism,* Oxford: Clarendon, 1982.

O'Hear, A. *Experience, Explanation and Faith,* London: Routledge, 1984.

Peterson, M. et al *Reason and Religious Belief,* 3rd. ed. New York; Oxford: Oxford University Press, 2003.

Plantinga, A. *Warranted Christian Belief,* New York; Oxford: Oxford University Press, 2000.

Quinn, P. and Meeker, K., eds. *The Philosophical Challenge of Religious Diversity,* New York; Oxford: Oxford University Press, 2000.

Ramsey, I. *Religious Language,* London: SCM, 1957.

Ross, J. *Portraying Analogy,* Cambridge: Cambridge University Press, 1981.

Schellenberg, J. *Prolegomena to a Philosophy of Religion,* Ithaca, NY: Cornell University Press, 2005.

Stump, E., ed. *Reasoned Faith,* Ithaca, NY: Cornell University Press, 1993.

Swinburne, R. *The Existence of God,* 2nd. Ed. Oxford: Clarendon, 2004.

Swinburne, R. ed. *Miracles,* New York; London: Macmillan, 1989.

Wallace, S. ed. *Does God Exist?: the Craig-Flew Debate,* Aldershot: Ashgate, 2003.

Index

Biblical and apocryphal references